CW00319010

CELEBRATING 50 YEARS OF **SkandaVale**

1973 — 2023

We dedicate 'The Spark Becomes Fire' to Guru Sri Subramanium, founder
of Skanda Vale and our eternal companion. Also to Community members past
and present and countless devotees who have given of themselves to help
make Skanda Vale the sacred and beautiful place it is today.

It is only through Guru's grace that this book has come into being.

THANKS

Our special thanks to Charice Bhardwaj who worked tirelessly with great dedication in bringing the book from inception to life. Thanks to Elsa Benoldi for her infinite patience in helping to develop the design work. To Lucia Rivera Van Houwelingen, a budding young artist, for her illustrations. Also to Joseff Howells, Maanasa Visweswaran and Joanna Prychard for proofreading and glossary.

Thank you to all Community members and devotees who have also contributed in so many ways and collectively have brought these pages so vibrantly alive.

All proceeds from the sale of this book support the work of Skanda Vale Hospice, where we care for families affected by life limiting illnesses, free of charge.

Published by: Skanda Vale, Llanpumsaint, Carmarthen, SA33 6JT.
© 2023 Skanda Vale. All rights reserved.

No part of this book may be used or reproduced in any manner whatsoever without permission. No part of this book may be stored in a retrieval system or transmitted in any form or by means including electronic, electrostatic, magnetic tape, mechanical, photocopying, recording, or otherwise without prior permission in writing of the publisher.

For information: enquiries@skandavale.org

First Edition: December 2023.
Printed by Gomer Press, Llandysul, Wales.
Set in Meta Serif Pro.

CONTENTS

FOREWORD

Skanda Vale—the very name brings a refreshing feeling of peace and unsullied joy in the minds of all those who visited this beautiful ashram in Wales. Many beautiful memories. Everybody who came there went back with their hearts full. Nobody ever left Skanda Vale disappointed and empty-hearted.

The silent, witnessing face of Guru Subramanium keeps reappearing in the mind's eye. The force behind Skanda Vale. The energy behind it all. The medium through which Lord Skanda and Mata Kali manifested there. The one who brought Lord Ganesha, Maha Vishnu as Sri Ranganatha, as well as beings of different species and all the human beings who came there. One can only remember Him with deep love, respect and deep gratitude. This was the man who, with His power of Intention, manifested Skanda Vale as we see evolving now.

We are born into noises. We are used to noises. We believe noises are natural. When we continuously live with the illusion that noises mean truth, a wise man happens, who tells us otherwise. He comes to tell us what we never imagined— that noises are our foster state and that we belong to silence. This usually shocks us as we do not and cannot perceive this as a reality. Wise men repeatedly remind us, and through various methods and means they prove to us, that we have come from silence and noises are only unavoidable expressions of terrestrial existence. They also tell us not to be deluded by sounds. They create spaces for us to calm down and reduce our inner noise levels and start feeling our original state. We realise, sounds are from us, but they are not us. We do not belong to sounds.

We belong to silence. Eventually, we start being silence and we become one with the master. All separations that sounds maintained dissolve and we become a large volume of silence. We come back home.

This is the journey, or rather, a detour of human existence. We are celestial beings, highly intelligent and pure, walking the earth in the garb of human beings. When we realise what we are, the show ends there. Then, all that we perceive is uncontaminated unity. Spaces like Skanda Vale are to facilitate and ease this journey to oneself.

Fifty years is a milestone. It is not just the manifestation of the sankalpa of the Guru, but also is the developing aspiration of many people who use it as a platform for their highest discipline and eventual transformation. Skanda Vale will and should live on to nurture and strengthen many beings of Kaliyuga in their ultimate pursuit of liberation from their native patterns as well as the inherent birth and death cycle of existence.

— BRAHMARISHI MOHANJI

INTRODUCTION

Guru would say 'It is only in the silence of our own thoughts we will discover God, not in the hubbub of worldly activity.' Initially, I took this to mean that when we sit quietly in contemplation, inner prayer, meditation, desisting from the physical and mental activity of our daily lives doing things, we will discover God.

Slowly I came to realise that whenever we own an action, we think we are the ones doing things, our ego is involved and this results in karma, the requirement for fulfillment, completion, whether the action is perceived as good or bad. It is only upon experiencing we cannot do anything—that the Divine is the doer and that our sole requirement is to become unconditionally available, that we become a pure channel and medium used to facilitate the unfolding will of the Divine.

'In the silence of our own thoughts...' is actually a thought-less state; total inner silence, satchitananda, timelessness. An experience of absolute, not relative, truth where there is complete awareness that the myriad experiences of our worldly existence are but a grand illusion.

Through grace, the worshipper integrates totally with the one who is worshipped. The karma yogi becomes the spontaneous expression of unconditional love in service to the Divine embodied in every life form. The jnani connects directly to the source and expresses the highest absolute truths delivered with a clarity born of direct experience, not intellectual understanding.

An opportunity presents itself to those who read this book, to actually walk with Guru, to connect to his consciousness. The truths that are expressed are absolute.

If we are open, empty and do not allow the rational mind to interfere we can be led on a journey to complete inner silence.

Guru never spent hours discussing the finer points of spirituality, but as a pure instrument of the source, of God, transformed those whose lives he touched with the power of his presence and practical example of his life. His every moment, word, action, touch, bhav, or seemingly throw-away comment, has a purpose and is infused with power. Nothing is coincidental or haphazard.

Through the dramas and divine theatre enacted in establishing Skanda Vale, Guru sets out some of the qualities we need to cultivate if we are to tread the path of fire, to liberation. Utter conviction, single-mindedness and the clear sankalpa of a divine purpose delivered by one who gives of himself totally in service to God and wants nothing from the earth. Emotions, attachments, expectations of society and family have no bearing on the purpose.

Guru emphasised it is the birthright of every person to directly experience God. His life and Skanda Vale provide this opportunity to countless souls. It is with immense gratitude to Guru and the Divine that we offer the pages that follow. May they help ignite that presence of God so the spark becomes fire.

— SWAMI SURYANANDA

01. SRI LANKA

Our story begins with a remarkable and mischievous young boy who was born in Colombo, Sri Lanka in 1929.

I was given the most ridiculous name of Percival. This, I thought, was the greatest insult to my intelligence as well as anyone's imagination.

Naturally cheeky and unusually quick-witted, Guru was quite a handful for both his parents and teachers.

GURU SRI SUBRAMANIUM: I don't want to give the impression that I was a holy little child from birth. On the contrary, I was the most naughty person you could have found, so much so that when I was driven to school by the chauffeur, I would immediately go off with friends on a razzle and come back in time to be picked up by the chauffeur in the evening. My father, therefore, had a lot to put up with and this went on for quite a while until one day, he said to me, 'I haven't read a report from your school in a long time.'

I had already told him that I was fed up with school and wanted to leave, but he had insisted that I continue with my studies. When he mentioned the report, therefore, and asked me why he hadn't seen it, I didn't want to tell him a lie. 'Well,' I said, 'why don't you go and find out?'

He arrived at the school and to his absolute horror, was informed by the Principal that his son had left about two years previously.

JUSTIN: He spent very little time in school and most of the time, he spent in the cinema... They had so little to teach him anyway, and he was constantly correcting his history teacher about the real facts of whatever event they were learning, which caused huge tension.

Guru could never understand why he must take his teacher's words for truth, when in his mind's eye, he could go to that historical event and experience the reality himself, all without reading a single book.

St. Josephs College — Colombo.

TOP: Guru attended the Catholic St Joseph's College in Colombo.
BOTTOM: 'Shanti' — the family home where Guru grew up.

'Oh, life is a bore!' I thought, 'I must leave it all and get on with my own way of thinking!'

GURU: I couldn't explain that I already possessed such an inheritance of knowledge within myself... to be educated like that was not necessary because I already had inside me a wealth of education.

From a young age, Guru possessed an extraordinary ability to relate to the forms of life around him. Whether it was Monty, his Jack Russell, or the children at school, having such an intimate understanding of others made him acutely aware of their sorrows, needs and joys. He especially loved the company of birds and animals, whom he related to more like friends.

LEFT: Guru's family home was always full: friends, children colleagues, patients, servants, relatives... it was a lively place.

GURU: I had a marvellous collection of doves and I converted a whole garage to keep them. One of them was a wonderful little bird called Aska. He had beautiful red eyes and was absolutely adorable. If he saw me from a distance, he would fly over and land on my shoulder. He would then go round and round talking to me, as if saying, 'How nice to see you!' If he saw me arriving in my car, he would fly across and follow the car until it halted and I got out.

Sometimes, though, he would go absent; he would disappear and I knew there were many hawks and buzzards in the vicinity that could kill him. I would then write a little note to St. Francis asking for his help. 'Please look after my Aska because he is such a friend.' However, this dove was a far wiser young man than I because he was after the girls! He used to go to other collections of doves and pigeons and come back every so often with a new young lady.

Guru kept a second flock of pigeons at his holiday home in Galle. When the summer ended and it was time to return to Colombo, he naturally wanted to bring them all home. Much to his mother's astonishment, he would stand beneath the flying pigeons and catch them gently in mid-air. His mother would ask how he could handle them so tenderly, to which he replied, 'I read their minds, so I know exactly where they're going to fly.'

My mother asked me once why my friends would come to see me so early in the morning.

'They get shocks from me!' I told her.

'Shocks from you?' she said, surprised. 'Do you have some electrical connection in your bed?'

'No,' I replied. 'My body has electricity.'

So they would come, sit on my bed, tap me and get shocked. This was their experience. They didn't call it spiritual; they didn't know what it was. I didn't know what it was either; it was simply my nature to have this.

In the wind and trees, flowers, bugs and bees; everything had a vibration.

GURU: When looking at plants, in my mind's eye, I would bend down to the level of that plant and delve into its life pattern. I would stare, fascinated, at the little grubs, the beetles and flies, and all the minute plant life. If I saw a flower, I wanted to go deep within that flower to feel its vibration. The trees and plants, all of life, communicate with me. They literally talk to me. If they are in need, they tell me. If they are hungry or short of water or food, or if someone has cut a branch when they shouldn't have, they complain to me. They tell me everything. I don't have to go and ask anybody what is going on; I simply walk around and the plants tell me all the secrets that have happened around them.

We were a very caring and tightly-knit family. We had a lot of fun.

Guru had a deep love and respect for his mother. Mabel de Silva was a great seer and a formidable woman of her time. As warm as she was tough, 'Mummy' had spiritual power which she used to help people everywhere in Sri Lanka. In fact, her work was in very high demand.

GURU: Every morning, there would be a constant flow for what we called her 'surgery'. It was very amusing because my father had his [doctor's] surgery also and it was a common sight for us to see one line of people waiting to see my father and another, in the opposite direction, waiting to see my mother. To grow up in that atmosphere, witnessing science and spirituality develop side by side was fascinating for us as children.

RIGHT: Mabel de Silva with Guru's father, Dr. D.B.J. de Silva who was Head of Medicine in Sri Lanka. Guru said, 'One of his endearing qualities was that he had such love for his patients. I have yet to meet a doctor who matched his care.'

Guru accompanied Mummy on some exhilarating adventures as part of her work. He enjoyed their excursions together which were far from the humdrum of his school books.

JUSTIN: His mother took him to an abandoned Buddhist temple in the jungle, not far from Kataragama. She wanted to meditate inside but it was known to be protected by snakes because of the power that the temple contained. So, when Guru opened the old, corroded door, he found hundreds of cobras curling around the floor.

GURU: 'Now, don't move and keep quiet!' she said softly. 'They will soon all go, giving us room to enter.'

I was fascinated and kept digging my mother in the side. 'Look, look, there's one hanging from its tail!' My mother, though, didn't move a muscle and when a path eventually cleared, we stepped in.

My mother approached the Buddha, bent down and venerated him, totally ignoring the cobras. There I was, not so much scared as immersed in all the cobras that were hanging from a table just two feet away from me. When she had finished meditating, she stood up, waited and again, the snakes parted.

That was the extent of her immense bhakti, her devotion to the Divine. She was so sure that nothing on earth was going to disturb her when she wanted to worship the Lord.

My mother had power, real power, with which she could see black magic or bad vibrations.

JUSTIN: It was common practice in Sri Lanka to employ an expert in the dark arts to create disharmony in someone's life. Equally, there were people you could engage to remove such curses which might manifest as illnesses, business failures, obstructions to building works and so on. She never took money for it, but Mummy was one such person. She had this gift of purifying spaces of dark energies. It would often involve a site inspection and she would bring Guru along with her! They were totally protected, so there was nothing to worry about in that respect. She would take his hand and ask him 'Where do you think the problem is?' and Guru would sort of sniff it out! He always said that this was part of the training he received from his mother, this ability to see with his third eye. The more he did it, the more his confidence improved and he ended up rather enjoying these trips. I can just see the two of them now, setting off for another job!

GURU: Even during those early days she had tremendous vision and that vision was accompanied by humanity. Her warmth and humanity was something really worth seeing because it embraced everyone who was drawn into her orbit. I can remember her adopting, during my childhood, at least twenty children, and they were all eventually given in marriage.

She had this incredible vision and knowledge, as a great yogini, that God was omnipresent and omnificent, manifesting in all religions.

JUSTIN: His mother's temple was absolutely beautiful. Built for her by a great man in Colombo in the garden. It was six-sided like a hexagon with a tiger skin in the middle and on each wall, a different facet of the Divine—Christianity, Buddhism, various Hindu facets—and depending on the time of year, she would simply rotate on the tiger to face the relevant aspect. I'd be intrigued, it seemed like such a clever way of doing it.

She would walk around the temple talking aloud to the different aspects about everything in her heart—her concerns, her prayers, all the private, family issues! Anyone close by could hear everything, of course, but she never seemed to mind because that was her relationship with God.

RIGHT: Mummy welcomes a wandering sadhu to her temple.

I loved his simplicity and purity—his love and recognition of the presence of God in all of life.

GURU: St. Francis of Assisi worshipped the Lord in the sun, the moon, the stars, and all of Creation. That is how a human being should really worship the Lord. Because the Lord permeates the whole universe; in the plants, the trees, the birds, the fruits—everything.

I could see the Lord, and not only the Lord but great saints like St. Francis and St. Anthony of Padua as well. I could talk with them, share my thoughts with them and tell them everything I wanted.

I had this feeling that here was a wonderful saint, St. Francis of Assisi, who was not for the rich but for the poor. He recognised the sanctity of life in all of life and praised all of Creation. I could relate to this because I felt exactly the same and looked upon the animals that I kept in the same context.

Yes, I was born with a golden spoon in my mouth.
But, like St. Francis and the Buddha, I spat it out.
It was a total obstruction for me to do God's will.

GURU: We would pass the little huts in the hamlets by the roadside and in my mind, I would go into those huts and think about how those people were living; whether they were hungry and if so, where their next meal came from. Those people, for me, were paramount in my thinking because I knew how difficult it was for them to survive. They were poor, very poor, but they were beautiful people. The salt of the earth.

I was concerned because I was privileged and I knew that other people weren't, so this drama went on all the time. My constant wish was for something better for us, for all of mankind, than what we had now. Suffering has a meaning for every human being, so why was I born like this with all these privileges? I must somehow use them for our wellbeing.

'The time will come when you will take My name and from now on, I will guide you. The only condition I lay before you is that you do not take a penny from any human being on My behalf.'

– LORD SUBRAMANIUM

Following the instruction of the Lord to 'take His name,' when he was only nine years old, Guru changed his name from Percival to 'Subra.'

GURU: I had a sense of feeling that I knew quite a lot. This, though, was something that I could not share. People just couldn't understand. Nobody that is, except my nanny who used to come to my room, a little annex room that was full of lamps and pictures of the Divine where I did my own pujas. I had my own shrine and I had a pretty good idea about what the Lord wanted me to do because my relationship with God was quite distinct.

If you could only imagine somebody so highly sensitive having to cope with the mundane itty-bitty rubbish that people are involved in. Between the age of seven and twelve years, I became more and more inward. I wanted to be close to myself, even whilst I played with people. If things were happening that were not gentle, sweet and beautiful, then it jarred. It jarred tremendously and I pushed everything away.

41

Guru's close link with the Lord didn't stop him from enjoying life as a young person. He attended dances with friends, led a musical ensemble that toured across Sri Lanka and ventured into the jungle in search of a cheetah to keep as companion for him and his dog.

Being with people who were spontaneous and who had a lot of love and laughter —this was another side to my spiritual life that was so wonderful for me because I never disassociate God from my living.

I think it would be a marvellous idea if I took the first ship out of Sri Lanka!

Guru loved his life in Sri Lanka but something in him longed to journey further, have adventures and experience all the world had to offer.

GURU: I was ever so excited about leaving because for me, it was an adventure waiting. At the same time, it was heart-wrenching knowing the permanency of what I was doing. I was a young man moving away not only from all the luxuries of life, but also from the sentimental attachments to the things he loved the most. I was leaving behind my animals, which had been my best friends.

'You are crazy!' my mother said. 'You have so many lives around you.' I had a job to do, though. From an early age, I knew I had to go and make my way in the world; to go and find solutions to the problems of life that people had. I had to break all the bonds of attachment I had in order to go and serve God. This was the inner part of my commitment to Him. I couldn't discuss it with my parents. I couldn't discuss it with anybody because spirituality is about yourself and God.

Rambawe

Damboul

Chilon

Karnegalle

Matella or
Ft McDowal

Kaloday

Maravilla

Negambo

Bintenne

Kandy

Eraril
Karrewau

Kottan
okenee

Ambopusse

Patipal

Pedaratallagalla

Baddoolla

Nalnoonacooly

Singaretop

Yuwerra
Ellia

Kaude Vol

Walfloooler

COLOMBO

Chaddewahr

Arookjam E

Apperetotte

Adams Peak

7420

Pantura

Kerijalle

Kaltura

Halnapura

Balmeden

Jakelle

Little Basses

Barberyn

Herisa

Gampala

Palatupane

Great Basses

Bentotte

Bondgalle

Amblangodde

Dunmolla

Hambangtotte

Kalametta B

Pt de Galle

Belligam

Tangalle

80

Matural

81

82

C E Y L O N.

Leaving Sri Lanka, therefore, was truly one of the most dramatic moments of my life. I stood there alone on the ship deck, watching the land of my childhood slowly recede into the distance.

GURU: 'Everybody is going to say goodbye to me on the jetty and nowhere else. I don't want all that sentimental tosh on the ship!' They were all absolutely heartbroken, but I was so joyful! 'Now, I'm my own master!' I said to myself. 'This is when life begins in earnest.'

RIGHT: Guru bought a single pass aboard the Stratheden, which would sail from Australia to London.

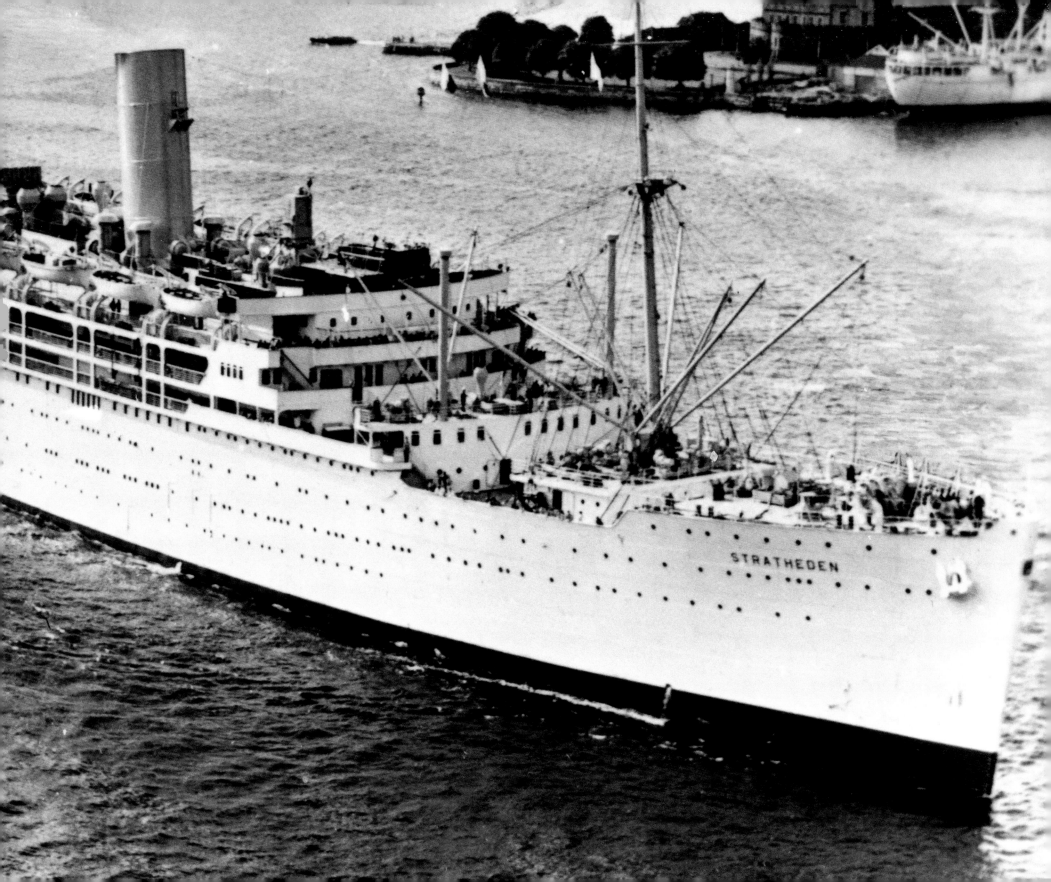

Guru's voyage on the Stratheden unfolded like any great adventure story, filled with new friends and characters who opened his eyes to new experiences and ways of living.

What made the journey so enjoyable was the young Australians I met who took such an interest in me. For the first time, I felt quite grown up. I made friends quickly, easily and soon, we were having a riotous time together.

LEFT: Guru (centre) on deck with the Australians.
RIGHT: Guru and friends (third from right).

There is a photograph of
me in a dinner suit being
greeted by the Captain.
It is the furthest thing from
what anybody would ever
imagine a spiritual being
to be wearing. This, though,
is exactly the theme
I pursued in my life, and
should never be forgotten.

But being immaculately dressed
was not as effortless as he thought.

GURU: For some extraordinary reason, these people were very keen to know what I did with my clothes after they had been worn. This was because every day, they saw me wearing something different that was beautifully washed and pressed. Now, I had never, ever washed a garment in my life. Not a shirt, not even a handkerchief. I'd never done anything for myself as a young man except have fun.

'Come on,' they said, 'we had better show you what to do with them!' and then took me to the ship's laundrette where they got all my stuff washed. They began to educate me that life had to be worked at—it didn't just happen. I learnt about washing clothes and then, of course, I had to be shown how to iron them which was even funnier, but I enjoyed every minute of it. It was a challenge and a change from my earlier life.

People were fascinated by Guru; his speech, his smile, his colour, his whole manner of being—sometimes people even waited outside his hotel to see him.

'Sir, the way you walk and talk, you must be a prince!' they said. 'Could you tell us who you are?' 'I am the Prince of Nowhere!' I replied. 'Ah,' they said, nodding their heads, 'the Prince of Nowhere!'

GURU: I had not the slightest idea what it meant to travel around with so much luggage and there was nobody to advise me on what to do. There I was, arriving like the great Raj with seven massive cases following me.

I visited almost all the European countries as a tourist.

GURU: I was fascinated by European culture—the paintings, the music, the drama and the people. I love people; the way they live, the way they conduct their lives. I used to just stand and listen to them talking, or go to theatres and meet up with new acquaintances. I spent much of my time doing that. In Italy, I would sit out in the piazzas sipping a black coffee and experiencing life. In Paris, I would sit in the cafés listening to music, or walk beside the Seine. Edith Piaf was very popular in those days. I admired her not just for her talent, but also for what she represented. I could see what she saw in France: the great divide between the rich and the poor, and she was its bridge. She was a great artist.

TOP: Visiting the Colosseum in Rome.
BOTTOM: The tomb of St. Cecilia, patron saint of music —
Guru had a strong desire to pay respects at her shrine.

> At every leg of my journey, someone was there to greet me, look after me and take me into the heart of local culture and society.

GURU: I went and spent a month in Rome and there, I met the Archbishop of Sri Lanka who took me around the whole of the Vatican. Because of him I was also taken to the Catacomb of St Peter's Basilica, where the nuns and priests care for the living saints. These are the sacred relics of the church that the public are never allowed to view and the guide takes you very carefully through this passage, making sure nothing is touched. The atmosphere was extraordinary. It is not one of decay; it is one of suspension of time. Seeing them like that, laid out on catafalques, you thought them to be asleep so you found yourself tiptoeing about not wishing to wake them up.

I have been exceedingly privileged. People were always there helping me, showing me the most sacred places in Rome so that I could worship in them. I have been given opportunities in most religions to relate to the highest realisation of God in man. You have one experience, then another and another; you can walk through a passage of time like the Catacomb, or churches and temples that are opened to you, see relics that are exposed to you. You seem to always be there at the right time. Time and timing is very important for the human being who is evolving spiritually. This is what rasmi, or divine light does; it opens the doors of opportunity for the person to worship God in His entirety.

LEFT: Archbishop Thomas Cooray, a friend of Guru's mother, travelled with Guru on the Stratheden. They met up again in Rome.

JUSTIN: I remember him describing the horrors he saw in Europe—he went to Hamburg and there wasn't a building standing. 'It smelt of death,' he said. He watched the people building back their lives, brick-by-brick from the rubble. Reconstructing entire cities.'

RIGHT: Guru was moved by the ration queues and 'Trümmerfrau' (literally translated as rubble woman) who, in the aftermath of World War II, helped reconstruct the bombed cities of Germany and Austria. With so many men dead or prisoners of war, this monumental task fell, to a large degree, to the women.

JUSTIN: He actually went to Nuremberg to sit in on the trials and listened first-hand to all those despicable crimes.'

JUSTIN: He was determined to witness the death and destruction that had been wrought by mankind to their fellow human beings. The Lord had sent him to do this.

Guru never lived on second-hand knowledge and he encouraged us to do the same. He read nothing and experienced everything. He would say, 'When you experience something, it's yours forever. No one can take it away from you.' And it was so poignant and alive in his mind, the futility, the suffering, the pointlessness of this war. I think that's what really pushed him towards the idea of forming a Community where people could serve mankind.

LEFT: The Nuremburg Trials ran from 1945 to 1949, during which hundreds of Nazis were tried for war crimes.

03. LONDON

I had been travelling in Europe almost two years before I finally made my way across from Calais to Dover and took a train to London.

GURU: Upon entering the carriage, I sat down and found myself surrounded by a wall of newspapers. I couldn't believe it. Nobody spoke to one another. No one smiled. Everybody seemed so glum and dull. On top of this, London was really grimy because in those days we had a lot of smog that you don't get now in Britain. Such was my first impression.

It was quite extraordinary really and gave me a severe jolt. Here was a place where I wanted to settle down because knowing the language was such an asset, yet the people were so, so insular. When I had been travelling about and living in Europe I had had such a different experience. There, people had been so exuberant and welcoming but here, the English didn't seem exciting at all. They seemed, though reliable, only very staid in their ways.

RIGHT: Commuters in the smog at Waterloo Bridge.

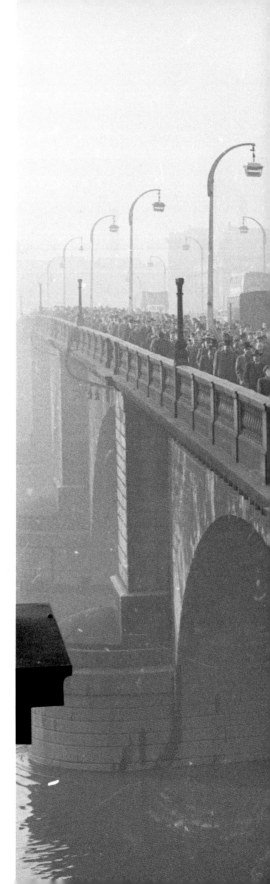

When I came to London, I felt as if I was a pioneer.

GURU: You could walk down Oxford Street or Regent Street, and you wouldn't see a coloured face at all. I was a pioneer and felt I was a pioneer, because I had come to start a new movement of educating and showing people in the West that we had something to offer them that they had not got.

A lot of people say 'these foreigners' but nobody can understand that, though we are not British we are associated so closely with, and look forward to the success and wellbeing of, the people in Britain. We are not thinking in terms of what we can get out of Britain, but what we can give, what we can contribute.

LEFT: Guru and Zigi, a friend from Hamburg.
RIGHT: A publicity shot—Guru worked as a film extra and, years later, compèred a show called 'Value for Money' for Southern Television.

I came to Britain with a lot of excitement about music
and theatre because these were things that I loved.

THE STAGE

Established 1880

EDITOR:

Eric Johns

Offices: 19-21 Tavistock Street, London, WC2E 7PA
(Open 9 a.m. to 5 p.m. Monday to Friday)
Telephones: 01-836 5213.
Telegrams: The Stage, London WC2

Subscription Rates (inland and overseas surface mail):
Year £4, six months £2, three months £1. Single copy
by post 8p. Air Mail rate on application.

THURSDAY, MARCH 16, 1972

INVOLVEMENT

THERE SEEMS TO BE A CRAZE these days to get audiences
more and more involved with the players taking part in the
productions they go to see. Informality is taken to the limit
at Newcastle University Theatre during Michael Bogdanov's
presentation of "Faust — an Experiment," being performed
in the Gulbenkian Studio. The production sets out to explore
the Faust legends and it also seems to explore a new and
closer relationship between the actors and their audience.

During a ballet performance at L'Institut
Français, Guru met a charming couple...

GURU: During the conversation, they asked me why I had
come to Britain. 'Because I love the theatre,' I told them.
'I am hoping to spend as much time as I can getting to
know it.'

'Well, I've got your address,' Mr Johns said. 'I will be
sending you tickets every week. You can come and review
all the shows with me and whenever I am going to the
theatre, I will take you.'

So began the most incredible excursion into the theatre
life of Britain and for the next four years, I saw almost every
show in the West End.

We were exclusive, we were expensive, but we were the best.

GURU: I met others I had known in Sri Lanka who were also interested in music and the arts. We thought we could contribute something to the people of Britain—Nimal Mendis on the piano, Mano Chanmugham on accordion, Anura on the drums and myself, and we would practise every day at the Centre for various shows we did to make some money. We called ourselves 'The Kandyans' and it wasn't long before we became a group that was really worth listening to.

LEFT: Nimal Mendis. **RIGHT**: Nimal and Guru.
OPPOSITE PAGE: The Kandyans played upbeat Latin American music in nightclubs, parties and debutante balls across London and beyond. Soon, they became known as the 'Debs Delight.'

A lot of people ask me, 'How did you follow a spiritual path and at the same time be in the theatre?'

GURU: It was very easy because I had a demarcation line and I didn't allow anything to devalue it. I wasn't going to sell myself in order to get a particular contract; I would have had no self-respect if I did. For my own spiritual purposes, I wasn't going to do it and I had this wonderful feeling that we were being successful, yet at the same time we hadn't changed any of our values.

RIGHT: Hélène Cordet, actress and owner of The Saddle Room nightclub in Park Lane, where The Kandyans had a residency. **OPPOSITE PAGE:** Guru and friends.

GURU: I stayed for about four or five years at Hyde Park Crescent and it was one of the most interesting and diverse times of my life.

A woman called Greta Valentine owned the house. The rooms were enormous and panelled in Russian oak, so the acoustics for practising singing were excellent. Also, in the lounges were two beautiful grand pianos made from rosewood. It was an artist's paradise—the great concert pianist Alexis Kligerman used to come and practise there.

Greta was a very kind person and would come rushing down the stairs to greet me when I returned from my work. 'Darling, I have made some food for you!' and she would have gone out shopping and baked some very nice cheese dishes. To get to my room from the front door would take me two hours or more because the place was full of different types of artists—when you returned from work in the evening, you just didn't know what to expect.

THIS PAGE: Greta Valentine—Guru's landlady and friend.
OPPOSITE: Ram Gopal—dancer and choreographer, was among the first to showcase Indian classical dance in the West, starting in the 1930s.

GURU: Living below my flat was someone called Ram Gopal and this man taught me all there was to know about artistic temperament. Ram was one of the most incredible people I have met in my whole life. He was a very great Indian dancer but the most undisciplined of human beings.

One day, he heard me coming downstairs and shouted out to me to come in to his flat. I entered, not knowing what to expect, and there was Ram, lying in his bath, holding court to a group of women. They were all standing around him and, to conceal his private parts, he was using a sponge that would from time to time float away.

Now, Ram was very much an actor and this sponge seemed to me very much part of the act. It was the funniest sight. He loved an audience and there he was shouting out to everybody, 'Darling, would you pass me the brush? Now, can you scratch me here?' and so on.

Everybody was a 'darling' to him and these were the people who sustained him in his life. They were all very aristocratic, wealthy women and he was in total command of their purses. His charisma was such that he had the power to literally mesmerise women.

This was the beginning of a period of almost thirty years of non-stop activity. I was young and resilient, a strong lad, and I thought sleep was a luxury.

GURU: It was a luxury because I was so excited by what was happening around me. It was also a very difficult time for me, because there was so much to do. I was quite literally working round the clock... I think the vitality and energy I got was from the Divine, otherwise I couldn't have continued like that in London for all that time.

JUSTIN: He worked at Selfridges in the day and went to the theatre at night. He would then come home, cook a huge meal and feed every person who had turned up for meditation and yoga. Only then would he actually begin teaching, by which point it was usually midnight. They would all go home around 3am and three hours later, he'd get up for work and do it all again.

LEFT: Guru and Joe Upton (right) with friends **RIGHT**: The Selfridges china department where Guru worked.

THE STATE APARTMENTS

ST. JAMES'S PALACE

(By gracious permission of Her Majesty The Queen)

CEYLON
INDEPENDENCE ANNIVERSARY
CONCERT

(In the presence of H.R.H. The Princess Royal)

Wednesday, February 5th 1964 at 8.00 p.m.

It was one of the most distinguished gatherings ever to come together at St. James'.

Guru, with Dr Malalasekara and actress Dame Flora Robson, compères a prestigious event at St. James' Palace in celebration of the 1964 anniversary of Sri Lanka's independence. Significantly, this was Guru's last appearance on stage—he felt the time was right to bow out of the theatre and focus on his spiritual work.

I hadn't come to convert people from one belief to another. I came to enrich people in whatever belief they followed.

GURU: These two old ladies came to me because they had nowhere to go—one of them was bankrupt and lived in the park. They chose meditation because they had heard all about it, but I think we were more like social services for them; they came for the hot soup and drinks, the love and care that I could give them.

I would say to Joe, 'Look, the old girls need a bath, let's go to the movies,' and we would go and sit through the most ridiculous films, complete nonsense. We often did this so that they could come and have a wash, then make something warm for themselves. We would then return back telling them how much we had enjoyed the films, which was very important.

ROBBIE: All sorts of people would gravitate towards him, and he would help them whether they were interested in learning about spirituality or not—it wouldn't matter. It was the human interaction that he was absolutely wonderful with and he would always take time with people; it was never rushed. Always full concentration on what they needed and what he could do to help. A very striking aspect of those days.

That was a most revolutionary period in Britain.

GURU: Many people came for the meditation and hatha yoga that I taught, and the vibration was lovely because of this. It was a continuous entrance and exit for people who wanted spiritual conduct and experience, as well as a training ground for our work in rehabilitating people who were drug pushers and users. We tried to help them come to terms with life because that was a most revolutionary period in Britain, the flower power days—people had become obsessed with drugs.

LEFT: 'Joy of Life' fountain, Hyde Park, 1967.

Every minute of the day I had to work so that, when people came to learn about following spiritual practices, we would be successful in not charging them money.

SISTER VAL: Guru had a contract to do the flowers for the Royal Variety Performance. I had no knowledge of floristry or anything and he was basically asking me to do the garland for the Royal Box. And I'm kind of like, 'What? Are you mad? This is ridiculous!' But again, there was that same energy from Guru 'You can do it, you know this, just do it. Get rid of the fear or the limiting thoughts, just go right ahead with it.'

And so, Party Flowers was actually a part of our lives. The energy of the place was so good, it was so 'anything and everything is possible. Everything's going to happen. It's all going to be just the most natural thing in the world.'

ROBBIE: He was running his business really cleverly and precisely, but he was always so detached and I think that's why he was so good at it because actually, he was one step away from it. He was doing it for a reason as a step towards Skanda Vale—and he never forgot that. It was never 'businessy'. It was a means to an end.

RIGHT: Guru outside Party Flowers—one of the shops that he and Joe Upton established to fund Guru's spiritual work.

ROBBIE'S DIARY, 01/73: Just back from Subra's. Beautiful meditation. He talked about the importance of awareness. 'Have your possessions but don't allow them to possess you, have your desires, but be the master. Conquer the ego; clear out the weeds and cobwebs with awareness and contemplation so that the flower can grow and come through the soil, open into the sun and call the light to shine upon it.' These are simple words but very, very deep in wisdom.

We sit at the kitchen table and talk. Every surface in the kitchen is covered with newspaper because the room is also an aviary. Huge numbers of various little birds fly free, perching on kitchen cupboards, ledges. Often you have to duck as one flutters by. Kitchen door must be opened and closed with care.

LEFT: Guru was known as 'Subra.' The title 'Guru' came much later.

ROBBIE'S DIARY, 01/73: One day, he asks me, 'What would you like? What can I do for you?' 'I would like to be more perceptive,' I say. He laughs. 'You have that already. However, when you next go for a walk, try to imagine extending your senses. Visualise your accustomed degree of perception as a box and try to push out beyond it.'

As I cross Cromwell Road half an hour later, I try to understand what he means. I visualise the box and reach out. By the time I reach the other side of the pavement, I have walked into a different world. A feeling of enormous peace and incredible perception. I look at the other people on the pavement and can understand them in a glance. My mind is clearer than mountain air, everything is profoundly self-evident and it is breathtakingly beautiful.

I walk the length of Kensington high street and back in this extraordinary state of mind... the sun is setting and slowly, I return to normal.

In the evening, as usual, I go to the temple. Subra opens the door. 'Well? Did you have an interesting afternoon?' He twinkles with that look that says 'I know exactly what has happened.'

Don't believe in God, experience God.

GURU: Again, during those days in Earl's Court, I had an experience that I would call a lifetime experience because it has stayed with me ever since. I had been out with my pals celebrating my birthday and when I returned to my flat, I found a pile of letters and telegrams by the door wishing me well. Picking them up, I noticed one was a cable from my mother. It was telling me that my father had died and she was awaiting instructions for the funeral.

Prior to this, just the evening before, I had been meditating in my shrine and Lord Siva had come; His hair was like an immense circular pile going to the heavens, it was the Ganga flowing on Him and down. He sat directly in front of me, looking at me, and as He did so He began to speak, telling me He was my father, my ancient father and that He had come to be with me. On saying that, He merged into my body. As I say, this experience has stayed with me, inside me. From that moment onwards I can see Him at any minute, at any time, in my life. When I am chanting the Tryambakam I can see Him, and it is a very special boon that He granted me.

This leads me to say something I have never said before: I left His side to come to the world as a rishi. By way of explanation, a rishi is one who is totally merged with God, so as a rishi I am directly connected to Him. People find it hard to appreciate this link that I have with the Divine. They think that whenever I want to talk to God, I have to go into some form of trance. That is not so. This great boon is still with me, though I have become a human.

SWAMI SURYANANDA: And from that moment onwards, if he was worshipping Siva, he would raise out his arms and put them on the knees of Siva. You would see him doing that in the temple. He would stand there, merging with Him, and you could feel the ripples of energy just flowing around his body as he was One with the universe.

DR. DORA FONSECA. Her generosity outstripped anything I had had from anybody. She was a mother to the community, really, and by that I mean not just us, but to many thousands of people. If I had any devotees who had a problem, I sent them to her. She would take care of them.

REV. DR. J. ROSS KEILLOR. He had been the chaplain to Field Marshal Montgomery during the war. He used to sit and tell us how his faith had been shaken to the core by the scenes that he witnessed. It was he who consecrated our first sacrament and I considered that as very much a privilege.

PROF. G. P. MALALASEKERA. He was a remarkable man because, not only did he hold such a high office in the diplomatic corps (he became ambassador both to the UN and to the USA), but he also wrote an encyclopedia on Buddhism—I don't think there was another Sri Lankan so well read and conversant on the subject. Furthermore, he was the most humble human being I have ever met in my whole life. He really practised his faith and showed people what humility meant.

LEFT TO RIGHT: Founding members of the Community of the Many Names of God.

BADULLA KATHARAGAMA DEVALAYA

In 1964, Guru embarked on a journey
to Sri Lanka with the purpose of seeking
the Lord's blessing for the establishment
of a place of worship in the UK. His
destination was the ancient temple
of Badulla Katharagama Devalaya.

GURU: When I first arrived in Britain, I brought with me just a few pictures for my shrine because I had been travelling in Europe, and I couldn't carry holy images in my suitcase. It was only much later on during my first visit back to Sri Lanka that I set about getting what I wanted. Since I had never had a murti of the Buddha, I meditated very much in the hope of getting one. Then, one fine day, I saw this image of the Buddha in my meditation. I could see it was in a shop in Kandy, so I left Colombo immediately and found what I had seen in that very same shop sitting on a shelf. This inspired me a lot. It meant that the things I wanted for the worship of the Community were not just going to be bought, but were going to be directed by the Lord for us to have in the temple.

Similarly, I had never had a murti of Lord Subramanium, so on a subsequent visit to Sri Lanka I told my mother how I would like to go and meditate in Lord Subramanium's Temple at Badulla. She also wanted to come, and I recall with such satisfaction how she prepared the most beautiful offering basket to take with us. Early one morning, therefore, we travelled to Badulla with some friends and were met by the pujari there whom my parents knew very well. Having done our prayers, we gave the basket to the pujari who took it in, where it was then offered. I then told him of my desire to go and meditate in the first room if he didn't mind. He, of course, had no objection to this, saying how happy he was to see my mother, so both my mother and I went inside, sat down and meditated for a while.

As I sat there, I asked the Lord whether He would come and be with me. He appeared and simply said that He would. He then appeared again, but this time accompanied by a three-headed cobra, and the cobra began asking me questions. 'What is it that you want from the Lord?'

'I want Him to come and stay with me,' I said, 'to go with me to Britain. I also want from Him His authority, and to have no problems establishing His temple.' The cobra regarded me quizzically.

'Why do you not ask anything for yourself?'

'But if I have the Lord, what else do I want?' I replied.

THIS PAGE: Guru and the pujari outside the temple. It was believed to have been built in the 1600's—the inner sanctuary is famously guarded by a real (flesh and blood) cobra.

97

I then very clearly heard the Lord's voice: 'As you have not asked for any wealth or any treasures for yourself, you will have Me throughout all of your life.'

I finished my meditation, got up and went to speak to the pujari. I explained to him what had occurred, that I had seen the Lord and He had granted a request of mine. I then asked the pujari to do something on my behalf.

'Would you please go into the temple sanctum sanctorum and find out for yourself what the Lord told me, rather than me telling you? When you have found out, you can then respond to my request.'

I asked this because I wanted confirmation for myself that what I had seen and what I had felt was not imaginary in any way. Even though it was the Lord who spoke to me, I am, by nature, very sceptical. I have to examine everything most thoroughly to make sure it is not some play of the mind.

The pujari was a very nice elderly gentleman. 'Why don't you go and have some lunch,' he suggested politely. 'In the meantime, I will prepare a special offering which I will take into the inner sanctum after you have returned. I will then do a special puja and come back to you.'

We followed his advice and went and had a meal, came back and the old boy took the offerings into the temple and there he did this incredible puja. I could hear him literally going into a trance. This carried on for about half an hour, then the chanting finally ended and he re-emerged not by himself but with all the authority that I wanted. He brought with him a vel, a small spear, wrapped in a betel leaf and, smiling broadly, he handed this to me saying: 'That is the authority of the Lord you asked for, and the Lord will come to be with you wherever you go!'

LEFT: Guru, Mummy and the pujari, outside the temple.

ABOVE: Guru at Vedihiti Kanda.

You can imagine how elated I was to have been granted the Lord's power and authority, yet I still didn't have an image of Him. 'There is one problem,' I told the pujari. 'I have no murti of Lord Subramanium!' Still smiling, and with a shrug of his shoulders, he replied: 'I've done the puja for you and the Lord said He will give you what you want.'

So, we left the temple and all returned to Colombo. On our arrival home, the most extraordinary thing happened: a lady arrived with an image of Lord Subramanium! She had made a vow that she would offer this murti to my mother's temple months ago, and she fulfilled her vow on the very day we returned. There and then, I also made a vow. 'Now that the Lord has given me all that I wanted and asked for, I shall make a pilgrimage to Kataragama itself.'

Close by to the temple of Kataragama is a hill called Vedihiti Kanda from where the Lord threw His Vel, and it was where the Vel landed that the temple was built. It was my desire, therefore, to climb this hill. Accompanied by my mother and Joe, my business partner, we arrived at its base, whereupon I took the murti out of the car and placed it on my head.

As I did so, a sudden tremendous cry arose from a great many peacocks, though we had seen none. It was as unexpected as it was thrilling, and their calls rang out as we began ascending the hill.

The day was very warm and there was no real pathway to follow, just a steep climb through dense jungle; you couldn't see anything but the bushes you clung to. It was the longest and most hazardous journey I had ever done, slowly pulling myself up, at the same time holding the Lord on my head. It was as if He was saying: 'I am going to put every weight upon you to see whether you truly want to fulfil that which you have asked for!'

As a prelude to this, whilst I was in London, I would see a yogi on top of this very same hill during my nightly meditations. He would be talking to me, so it was a wonderful moment as we reached the summit, after many hours of climbing, to be greeted by this yogi.

After welcoming us, I told him why I had brought the murti. 'Yes, I know!' he said, and took the murti from me and placed it on the rock altar from where Lord Subramanium had thrown the Vel. He then gave us refreshments and talked to us. Afterwards, he performed a puja and when he finished, he said:

'Now, go and take the murti from the altar, circle the rock three times and, without looking back, face the world and all the opportunities that await you!' As I picked up the murti and placed it once more on my head, temple bells began ringing down in the valley below as if prearranged. It was the most dramatic moment, straight out of some film script. To the accompaniment of the bells, Joe and I started down the hill and our descent was as if we were walking on air.

We found my mother waiting by the car and, after relating our experiences to her, I said: 'Now we have completed our journey, let's go to the river and have a bath!' Both of us were hot and sweating profusely, and our feet were boiling from walking barefoot, something I had not done for many a year, so I really felt as if I would never be able to walk again. However, when we reached the river and had a bath, all the pain vanished and, feeling completely refreshed and renewed, we returned to Colombo and then to Britain, where we began our work.

04. STARTING AN ASHRAM

JUSTIN: He wanted something very quiet and secluded where he could really almost be out of this world—it had to be a sort of a stepping stone between this plane and the next.

JUSTIN: He wanted to find somewhere rural. Somewhere where you could establish a monastery. It took quite a while, probably about a year. Every other weekend, he'd disappear on another mission up to Scotland, the home counties—here, there and everywhere but there was always something wrong. Often, for the owners, it was the colour of his skin. They'd say 'No, the property isn't available.'

Then the newsagents said, 'Have a look in the Farmers' Weekly, you never know what you might find.' That's where he spotted this tiny advert for a farmhouse. I remember him setting off, saying, 'I'm going to have a look at this little valley in Wales.' We all said, 'Pfft, good luck!'

But he came back from that trip with Joe saying that he'd basically bought it, which we all found rather extraordinary considering that Guru hadn't got a penny to his name! He had barely even looked at the house, but adored the seclusion of the valley, which was really important for the work he'd been charged to do. I think Guru pretty much made up his mind on the spot. He just knew it was right.

LEFT: Guru recognised that the land on which Skanda Vale now sits had a strong natural energy and that there had been worship here dating back thousands of years to pre-Christian times. **RIGHT**: The Farmers' Weekly advert.

JUSTIN: And when we arrived, I got a bit of a shock. I mean, it really was overgrown with brambles and neglect. And I remember when we got to the farmhouse itself, there were two sheep looking out at us from one of the top windows and chickens came running out of the front door.

It was a mammoth task, first of all in moving to Wales, then secondly, to establish ourselves as a community and become a charity.

ROBBIE'S DIARY 06/73: We pack the van, and then finally the car; the big statues, Nataraj etc on the back seat, in the boot, the others in every conceivable place... a row of little ones along the dashboard. The temple is empty. Guru goes in, looks around, then I slip in, determined to be last, and pause a moment there, remembering.

At the last minute, I am standing on the pavement about to wave them off, and he says 'Why don't you come too?' And I get in, in a t-shirt, with nothing but a drawing book. Guru, Justin and I all in the front, the statues everywhere else—it is one of those cars with a single wide front seat, the gear lever on the steering column, and we set off for Wales. Guru in very high spirits, drives down the motorway singing 'Gonna build a mountain.'

On the way, we pull into one of the service areas. As he locks the car I ask if I should stay with it, the statues are very visible: 'No one could possibly steal those statues.'

Finally we arrive, down the long drive, into the most chaotic farmyard—abandoned and rusty farm equipment and rubbish scattered around—everywhere a mess. The owners are still in the house for one more night, but chaos everywhere. Their pet sheep, Shelley, wanders from room to room. The accompanying van doesn't fit down the drive so we ferry everything into one of the barns. Countless journeys in a smaller van, and the piano by means of a tractor and trailer... everything hilarious.

We go for supper in a nearby pub; a lot of staring, and sleep in an old caravan that they had previously arranged to have delivered. Three of us in a row. In the morning Guru says, 'I just need to put some water on my eyes' and goes over to the tap in the courtyard.

The first morning at Skanda Vale.

GURU: When it became known that I intended to leave London, people thought I was committing suicide! They were extremely critical and were telling me how nobody would come to see me. 'Oh, this man has gone mad!' they were thinking. 'He is leaving a perfectly lovely business and lifestyle, and for what? To live in a derelict farmhouse in some remote part of Wales!' However, I obey the Lord, not people's fanciful concepts. I obey the Lord, and if the Lord tells me to do something I never question why, when or where. I follow it through.

LEFT: Guru worked hard to restore and renovate the derelict farm, whilst caring for an ever-growing number of animals.

ROBBIE'S DIARY 08/73: There is the house, a typical Welsh farmhouse, thick walls and slate roof, two rooms up and two rooms down, and a few ramshackle barns. On the right as you come in through the front door is the temple room, quite small but we can all just about fit in. The door on the left is the sitting room with the sofa and chairs from Earl's Court, the piano, and then the kitchen is at the back.

A muddy farmyard with machinery abandoned and rusting here and there, and a couple of caravans, one of which occupied by Brian and Sue. We sleep in our sleeping bags, higgledy on the floor in the left hand bedroom. Everything is relaxed, we talk with the Guru endlessly, make coffee, tackle various tasks.

I go sketching, explore the beautiful secluded valley. There is a place in the stream where we can have baths, except that twice a day an ancient train puffs by, halfway up the wooded side of the opposite hill. This is the only sign of civilisation.

And every evening—the temple. Guru starts speaking; always different things, from inspiration as it were, then he says a few beautiful prayers, the one about 'a triple blessing.'

Burn burn and destroy all that impedes the progress of these, thy devotees on their path to oneness with God. To their eyes greater vision, to their minds greater knowledge.

Guruji went to bed at seven this morning after spending the night looking for some people who took 16 hours to get here. They kept driving past, getting lost, breaking down... he fell asleep laughing hysterically at the memory of walking up and down a little Welsh village like a ghost.

Last day of the Subramanium ceremony—I have run out of clean shirts, the G notices. 'Here have one of my shirts.' and he hands me his best shirt; 'Oh no, Guru, this is your special shirt.'

'There is nothing special in life.'

RIGHT: The entrance sign reads 'Skanda Devale.' This was later changed to 'Skanda Vale' which has a double meaning, as Vale is both a valley and also Lord Murugan's 'Vel'—a spear.

Once I saw how young people wanted to come and join me, and not just on a visit but on a permanent basis, establishing a monastery became a possibility.

GURU: I had to give them the feeling, therefore, that we were not going to simply use them and kick them out. Towards this, I did my utmost to give them confidence that they were going to be a part of this whole establishment one day, when we could set it up more seriously. And people believed in what I did. They didn't need convincing because I put all my faith and trust in caring and looking after people.

Those who were at one time dropouts, and those who had wanted to follow a spiritual path, now had a real beginning, and they could follow it, but it was not easy going initially. That period in the life of this country when Skanda Vale was coming into being was a most difficult and undisciplined time. The people who were coming to see me at that time, and who wanted to live in the atmosphere of our community, often had very different ideas about spirituality.

Drugs were predominant in their lives, aimlessness was their forté, discipline was an alien subject, and they wanted things to happen without even moving a muscle. In their minds, everything should be possible, including thinking how spiritual they were, but they were unwilling to surrender their identity to God.

RIGHT: Tea and biscuits for Guru and Community members on the hay field.

SWAMI NARAYANA: Guru used to say that a monk should be so knackered that he had to crawl to his bed at night. In those days, we really did, I tell you.

SWAMI NARAYANA: A difficult career choice to begin life in an unformed ashram. It wasn't like a comfy monastery with cloisters and routine and everything laid out, hundreds of years of tradition. It was just hard work. Whether you understood what you were there for or not, it was hard work and you got on with it. And you either had faith in Guru or you didn't.

It was all to do with the importance of caring for life. If you've taken responsibility for life and responsibility for people, then you have to follow it through. Guru would quite often make us realize that we were on call 24 hours a day to the Lord.

LEFT: The work was outdoors and physically demanding.

I am essentially a Franciscan because
I love to serve the Lord in all His Creation
and here at Skanda Vale, there was an
opportunity to do just that.

GURU: All life is evolving towards God. If we could only give some measure of help towards all of life, then we would have educated ourselves to recognise God in everything. We would have educated ourselves to appreciate what hardship these life forces have.

As human beings, we have evolved to a level where we can understand and discriminate. We can cry out when in pain, seek the assistance of doctors, get clothing, shelter and food. But these lives outside of us are evolving too and it is our responsibility to assist them on their journeys; to care for them wholly as long as they live and right to the last breath.

All life is given by the Divine and it is not ours to take away from anyone. When this calf is old, it would be unpardonable of me to think of her as dispensable, to say, 'Well, she is old now, let us get rid of her.' No, we cannot and this is what I teach the monks. That is where loyalty comes into being.

THIS PAGE: Guru with Sisters Topsy and Trudy, Brother Ian and Jersey cows. The Lord Murugan Temple is in the background.

We lived almost one-hundred percent on what was offered and what was grown.

GURU: Looking back, those early days were all about making do because we had very little money. Self-sufficiency was important for our survival; the cows yielded milk and we grew vegetables. It allowed us to say to people who came to stay with us, 'We haven't got much; we are learning to build our resources and be self-sufficient.' It took time, but time was in our hands.

SWAMI NARAYANA: Not many visitors meant not many offerings. I used to make a jug of sweet tea for elevenses, which was eagerly awaited by the outdoor workers for a break and sugary fix. At some point, the cows stopped milking in order to calve, but the workers kept coming for the tea. Then the tea ran out, so I started using herbs. Still, there was demand. Then the sugar ran out. Soon, the number of customers for warm herb water dropped to near zero.

RIGHT: Guru, Community members and devotees make hay to feed the animals during the winter.

SWAMI NARAYANA: I don't see many people here today putting up with it—you had to have a particular frame of mind. But then, we were all mostly under twenty-five and had lots of energy. Those that didn't meet the challenge dropped away; only two monks remain in the Community from those early days.

LEFT TO RIGHT: Sister Topsy, Sister Annabel, Brother Justin (Swami Shanmukhananda), Guru's mother, Brother Noel, Brother Ian, Guru, Brother Henry (Swami Kamalananda), Brother Holger, Sister Rosemary, Brother Peter (Swami Karuna), Brother Kenneth (Swami Narayana), Sister Val, Sister Trudy.

In order to establish a centre such as ours, we have given up a lot. This was important because people here in the western world are so full of material wealth and possession. So, to bring to people the consciousness of a simple life, we ourselves have given up all such luxuries. The hallmark of Skanda Vale is simplicity; it is austerity, and through that austerity, we can discover, in the silence of our own thoughts, God.

GURU: I felt so elated to know that I could bring about a new expression of St. Francis' work through chastity, obedience and poverty.

THE COMMUNITY OF THE MANY NAMES OF GOD

Sri Sathya Sai Service Centre

FOUNDER PRESIDENT: BHAGAWAN SRI SATHYA SAI BABA

...NDA VALE, LLANPUMSAINT SA33 6JT DYFED WALES   Tel: PENCADER 421 (STD) 01559

CHARTER FOR THE BROTHERS OF THE COMMUNITY OF THE MANY NAMES OF GOD

Vows: Poverty
        Obedience
        Chastity

Brother Justin - temple and overall supervision
Brother Holdger - Maintainance of robes, bathroom and dairy
Brother Ian - Gown and Accounts
Brother Henry - London (for the moment)
Brother Tristram - Kitchen
Brother Kenneth - Goats, and often projects
Brother ...... - Chicken, gardening and projects

I know that the architect and design of all that is happening here in Skanda Vale comes from that first experience I had when I went to His temple at Badulla.

GURU: You have to have the authority of the Lord before you begin a temple. Yes, of course you can build a temple. You can put up any structure and call it a place of God. But for the Lord to give His personal approval, that this is something He wants established, is a different matter. I didn't want to just go building temples anywhere and everywhere, I wanted the authority of the Lord to do so. I wanted God to also reside there. That was how I felt inside me, and that experience was reassuring, knowing full well that we are not alone in Skanda Vale. We have got the Lord living with us here. It is a sanctuary for all of life— for many kinds of animals, all the strays, including the human ones, because it is the home of the Lord.

JUSTIN: He almost wasn't aware of what surrounded us, this hard reality on the ground, because he was living this vision of Skanda Vale and he could see what it was going to become. He could see that in a small matter of time, it would become a place of excellence, of immense spiritual value, where people could be close to God.

FAR LEFT: Guru raises the Vel flag at the start of the Subramanium Festival.
LEFT: The original entrance to the temple (now opens onto the Ganesh Terrace).

SWAMI NARAYANA: I used to really wonder, how is it that someone of Guru's stature could live in this derelict caravan? Or live with people like myself… a load of turkeys! I just couldn't understand it, but in retrospect, I can see very clearly that it meant absolutely nothing to him. Yes, he was capable of being very, very formal in his presentation; he could talk as easily to the aristocracy as he could to the farmer up the road, but his own position was actually neither here nor there. When you're really free, you don't care for status or comfort.

BROTHER ANDY: The early Subramanium festivals were held in a marquee at the back of the very small temple, and Guru would *become* Lord Subramanium—his face would become the same as the murti, exactly the same, as he carried the murti around on his head.

LEFT: Guru's caravan.
RIGHT: Subramanium Festival Reunion in the marquee.

Everything comes direct from God.

GURU: What people see being performed in our temples is what the Lord wants us to do, not what others want us to do. I am often challenged about this. We have many orthodox pilgrims and followers coming now to the temples, thousands of them, and when they see us performing rites many, many centuries old that we have resurrected, they want to know how this has come about. 'Don't ask me! Ask the Lord!' I tell them. 'It is the Lord that gave me directions. I know nothing!'

I am, though, an uneducated bum. I have read only one book in my life. In truth, all the knowledge that I have and reveal is what the Divine has revealed to me. I have no knowledge of the Vedas, except what the Lord tells me. I had no idea about mantras, tantras and yantras, nor the know-how to set up an institution such as we have here at Skanda Vale. My only source of information is the vast wealth of knowledge made accessible to me by the Lord Himself.

Nothing is secondhand. Everything comes direct from God. It is He who tells us, first-hand, how he wants us, in this age, to serve humanity and life. I am never alone, I am always with the Consciousness of the Lord, because the Lord is revealing everything to me—how the rituals will be performed—and as we go along, we perfect it.

SWAMI NARAYANA: When I first went inside [the temple] my feeling was that I was falling off the end of the world... just like this infinity opening up, in colour. There was just such a contrast between this enormity of experience... and this tiny room in the back of a derelict farmhouse.

LEFT: Shrines for Murugan, Buddha, Vishnu and Siva inside the temple.
NEXT PAGE: Word spread quickly and large numbers of devotees started visiting Skanda Vale on pilgrimage.

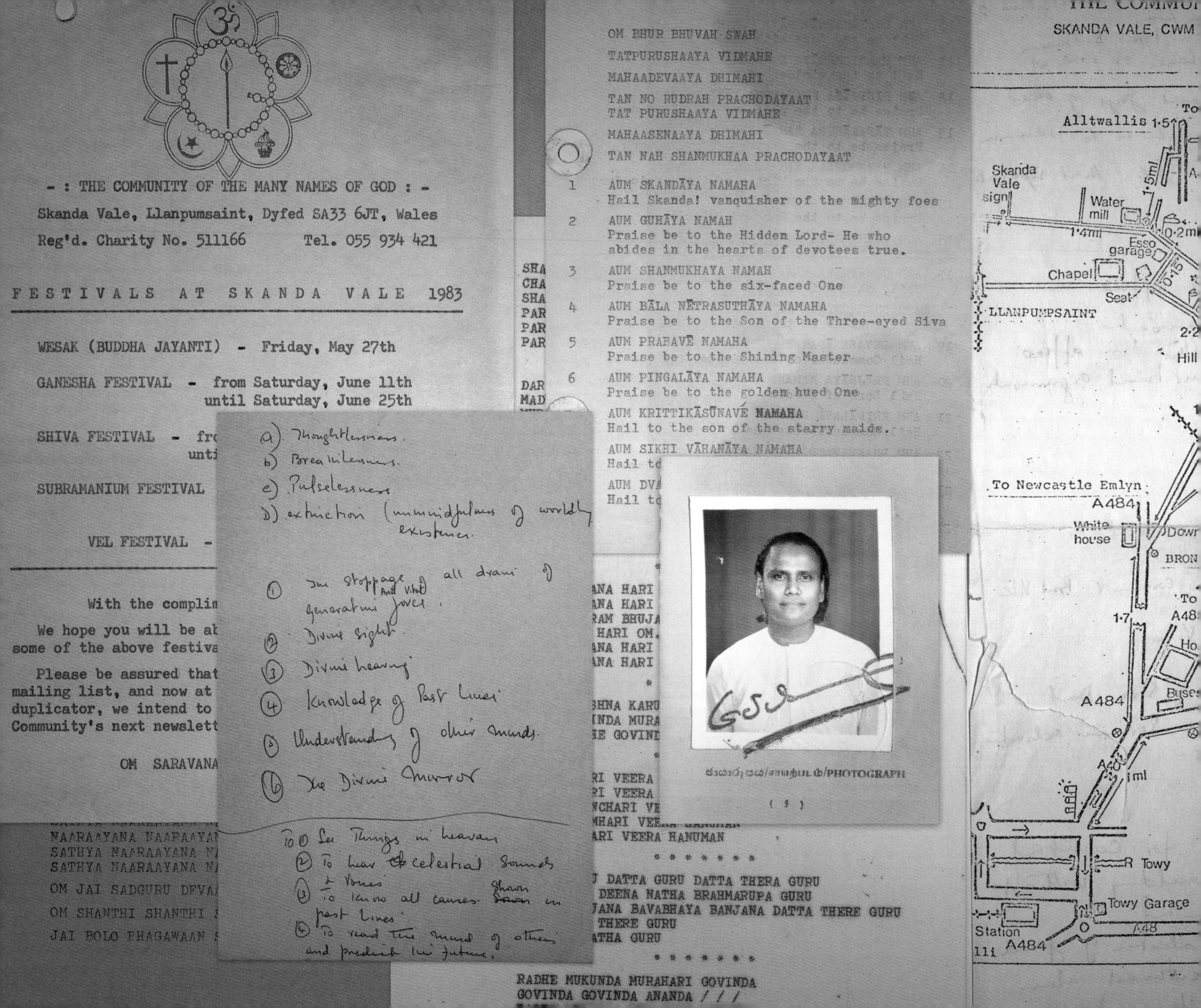

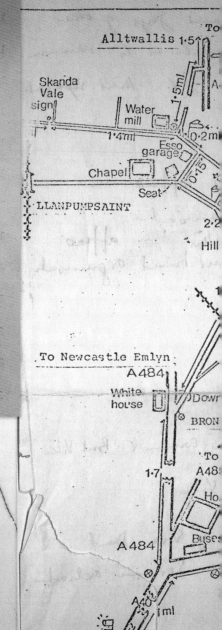

Document 1 (left, letterhead)

-: THE COMMUNITY OF THE MANY NAMES OF GOD :-

Skanda Vale, Llanpumsaint, Dyfed SA33 6JT, Wales

Reg'd. Charity No. 511166   Tel. 055 934 421

F E S T I V A L S   A T   S K A N D A   V A L E   1983
_____

WESAK (BUDDHA JAYANTI) - Friday, May 27th

GANESHA FESTIVAL - from Saturday, June 11th
                   until Saturday, June 25th

SHIVA FESTIVAL - fro
            unti

SUBRAMANIUM FESTIVAL

      VEL FESTIVAL -
_____

     With the complim

  We hope you will be ab
some of the above festiva

  Please be assured that
mailing list, and now at
duplicator, we intend to
Community's next newslett

      OM SARAVANA

NAARAAYANA NAARAAYAN
SATHYA NAARAAYANA N
SATHYA NAARAAYANA N

OM JAI SADGURU DEVA

OM SHANTHI SHANTHI S

JAI BOLO PHAGAWAAN

Document 2 (centre-top, typed verses)

OM BHUR BHUVAH SWAH

TATPURUSHAAYA VIDMAHE

MAHAADEVAAYA DHIMAHI

TAN NO RUDRAH PRACHODAYAAT
TAT PURUSHAAYA VIDMAHE

MAHAASENAAYA DHIMAHI

TAN NAH SHANMUKHAA PRACHODAYAAT

1   AUM SKANDAYA NAMAHA
    Hail Skanda! vanquisher of the mighty foes

2   AUM GUHAYA NAMAH
    Praise be to the Hidden Lord- He who
    abides in the hearts of devotees true.

3   AUM SHANMUKHAYA NAMAH
    Praise be to the six-faced One

4   AUM BALA NETRASUTHAYA NAMAHA
    Praise be to the Son of the Three-eyed Siva

5   AUM PRABAVE NAMAHA
    Praise be to the Shining Master

6   AUM PINGALAYA NAMAHA
    Praise be to the golden hued One

    AUM KRITTIKASUNAVE NAMAHA
    Hail to the son of the starry maids.

    AUM SIKHI VAHANAYA NAMAHA
    Hail to

    AUM DVA
    Hail to

ANA HARI
ANA HARI
RAM BHUJA
HARI OM.
ANA HARI
ANA HARI

SHNA KARU
INDA MURA
E GOVIND

RI VEERA
RI VEERA
NCHARI VE
MHARI VEERA HANUMAN
ARI VEERA HANUMAN

* * * * * * *

J DATTA GURU DATTA THERA GURU
DEENA NATHA BRAHMARUPA GURU
JANA BAVABHAYA BANJANA DATTA THERE GURU
THERE GURU
ATHA GURU

* * * * * * *

RADHE MUKUNDA MURAHARI GOVINDA
GOVINDA GOVINDA ANANDA / / /

Document 3 (handwritten note, centre)

a) Thoughtlessness.
b) Breathlessness.
c) Pulselessness.
d) extinction (unmindfulness of worldly
   existence.

① The stoppage of all drain of
   generative power.

② Divine sight.

③ Divine hearing.

④ Knowledge of Past Lives.

⑤ Understanding of other minds.

⑥ The Divine Mirror.

To ① See Things in heaven
   ② To hear the celestial sounds
      & voices
   ③ To know all causes shown in
      past lives.
   ④ To read the mind of others
      and predict the future.

Document 4 (right, map)

THE COMMU
SKANDA VALE, CWM

To Alltwallis 1.5
Skanda Vale sign
Water mill
Chapel
Seat
LLANPUMPSAINT
Hill

To Newcastle Emlyn
A484
White house
Down
BRON

A484
Buses

R Towy
Towy Garage
Station
A484
A48

Photograph caption

PHOTOGRAPH
(5)

GRAND VARIETY ENTERTAINMENT
IN AID OF

SKANTHA-VALE
(KATHIRGAMA TEMPLE, IN LLAMPUMPSAINT

PLACE:- ROYAL COMMONWEALTH-
18 NORTHUMBERLAND AVENUE
NEAREST TUBE — TRAFALGAR SQUARE

DATE - 28TH SEPTEMBER 74 (SATURDAY)

TICKETS:- £1·00 (OBTAINABLE FROM)

DR. DORA FONSEKA   373 - 6651
MISS CHANDRA SIRISENA.   542 - 4089
MR. P. SELVARAJAH   693 - 8687
MRS. D. WANIGASEKERA   542 - 7102
MR. SUSIL D. SOYSA   992 - 5149

PROJECT
CARMATHEN, SOUTH WALES (BUILDING FUND)

SOCIETY
LONDON WC2

GATES OPEN 6·30 PM STARTS 7·00 PM

MR K RAJASINGHAM   672 - 0579
MRS KENWORTHY   937 2107
"KATHIRAGAMA TEMPLE" PENCARDER 421
(SOUTH WALES)
PLEASE BUY YOUR TICKETS EARLY!
SEATS ARE LIMITED.

AUM

ABERGWILI

TEMPLE SERVICES & POOJ

Nightly at 9.00 p.m.
Sundays, Festivals & F
Days: also at 11.30 a.

ansea

RU SRI SUBRAMANIUM

te Hi
gazin
ay.
ected
at
e a
e a
t
ening
gh
with

live
nd
g;
n we
? We
y to
t
such
hich
w on
r at

least helped us to overcome the difficulties that we meet daily in
our living.

Don't let's allow 1980 to slip past, as 1979 did, without making
a real supreme effort to be organised and bring discipline into life.
Find time, make time, borrow time if necessary, but sit down quietly
with your self; be at peace with the world; and in that stillness
know that He is God.

OM   SARAVANABAVA   OM

Sister Annabel knew of the financial commitment Guru had made in order to establish Skanda Vale. One day she handed him a cheque large enough to wipe out all the outstanding debt.

GURU: She had written it out in my name. I had terrible fears about this. I didn't feel I had the right to accept such an amount of money so I referred it to the Lord. 'No, she wants to give it to you,' He told me. 'You haven't asked for it and you can accept it for the benefit of the Community.'

Having resolved my dilemma, I went and spoke to Annabel: 'Through your generosity, you have given us peace of mind and enabled me to pay off the balance of our bank loan. It allows us to set in motion the future of this Community—I therefore have no right to the ownership of this property any more and I shall now write to my solicitor asking him to begin the procedure of transferring the ownership to a trust.'

She believed in me and had the vision to see what Skanda Vale was going to be. Her trust in me gave me my freedom.

Ref. C8044

Alltwalis
Dyfed

Evans Bros.,

Have received instructions from the Executors to offer for sale by
Public Auction

The Freehold Farm

Known as

PEN-Y-GARN 68½ Acres

on Monday 13th November 1978

at 3p.m. at the Church Hall
Llanybyther (Mart Day)

(Subject to the conditions of sale to be there and then produced unless sold)

Situated ½ mile off the By-road and 1¼ mile in all from the main Carmarthen/Lampeter A458 Road, 3 miles from Llanpumpsaint Village on a different route from theFarm yard.

Farm House is stone and slated roof original built in 1843 and it is known to have been re-done in the early Century.

Accommodation:-

Living room with Louver Chimney. Kitchen, Parlour, 2 Bedrooms and single bedroom.

Rota Pump water supply from well on the ayrd. W.C. No Electricity.

Outbuildings:-

Stone and slated old type Cow House with wooden stalls, stone and slated 2 Pig Styes or Calf Pens, Stone and Slated stable, Barn with Loft, Cart House, Hay Shed.

Comprising in all 49½ Acres of Grazing and Arable Land easy to work, to add 19 acres of Woodland of Oak Growth, Goodfencing posts, in all 68½ acres or thereabouts.

With Vacant Possession on Completion

Further Particulars from Evans Bros., Auctioneers, Llanybyther Tel 444/5 Lampeter Tel 422395, Aberaeron, Tel 570462, Aberystwyth Tel 617016 or of the Acting Solicitors, Maessrs. Amphlett Lewis and Evans, Llandyssul, Tel 3244.

GURU: Both Sister Annabel and Sister Topsy played a prominent part in the formation and the work of the Community. Their generosity secured the land not only of Cwm-Creigiau Fawr but also later Pen-y-Garn, a far bigger farm at the top of the hill. They also made sure, through their wills when they died, that a very large sum of money, almost fifty thousand pounds, was available in shares so that we had an income to run Skanda Vale. These shares we still have, and we have been able to manage with the funds and donations that have been sent and given to us ever since.

LEFT: Cwm-Creigiau Fawr is the original name of the farm where the present day Lord Murugan and Sri Ranganatha Temples are. Pen-y-Garn is the name of the farm where the Maha Shakti Temple now is. **ABOVE**: Sister Annabel **RIGHT**: Sister Topsy.

JUSTIN: We knew we wanted to buy it [Pen-y-Garn] but didn't have a penny to spend. But when the property was finally put to auction, it went for more or less the same amount as the money which Sister Annabel had just come into. She had recently sold her house, liquidated her fortune and donated her entire wealth for the benefit of Skanda Vale. Divine timing was impeccable as we just about got the funds into place to bid on and purchase the farm.

The house was quite a mess.

JUSTIN: Having Pen-y-Garn meant that we could house and care for more animals, which we did. It was also Guru's first proper home in Skanda Vale. But the house was quite a mess—the moment we went in, the staircase collapsed into a heap of dust. We had to rebuild that and a few other things that kept going awry.

Just after we bought it, Guru's mother made her last visit and we drove her up in the Land Rover. She didn't get out, only looked at the house from the window and said, 'Hmm, well, you'll have a lovely time in there, my dear, because there are currently two residents whom you'll struggle to evict!' She was referring to two ghosts. So, usual story, lots of camphor, lighting lamps, some chanting. It took about six months before the atmosphere was beautifully cleansed and Guru could finally move in.

THIS PAGE: This small farmhouse at Pen-y-Garn is the present day Maha Shakti Temple.
NEXT PAGE: People, animals and views around Pen-y-Garn, circa 1978.

→2A →3 →3A →4 →4A →5 →5A →6

SAF.ETY FILM 5035 KODAK SAF.ETY FILM 5035 KODAK SAF.ETY FILM 5035 K

→7 →7A →8 →8A →9 →9.5 →10

SAF.ETY FILM 5035 KODAK SAF.ETY FILM 5035 KODAK SAF.ETY FILM 5035 KOD

→3 →3A →4 →4A →5 →5A →6

→30A → 31 → 31A → 32 →32A → 33 →33A → 34

KODACOLOR II FILM KODAK SAF.ETY FILM

→ 34A → 35 → 35A → 36 → 36A

In 1981, Valli the baby elephant arrived.

She had a floppy trunk, two twinkling eyes, and enough personality to keep Swami Karuna busy for the next four decades. She was the first temple elephant in Skanda Vale, fulfilling one of Guru's aspirations to keep and care for an elephant in the ashram. It is known that these stunning, highly-evolved creatures serve to purify a space and act as living representatives of Lord Ganesha; the elephant-faced God who embodies ultimate knowledge. Valli was born in the wild in Sri Lanka but was orphaned as a baby. She was found sheltering with a herd of water buffalo who took her in and cared for her. Valli was brought to Pinnawala Elephant Orphanage where the President of Sri Lanka gifted her to Guru. She lives in Skanda Vale with other elephants and her keepers.

SWAMI KARUNA: I wrote to my mother on the day Valli arrived. 'At last,' I said, 'I'm a Mother!'—I love mothers. My softest spot in the world is for mothers. I see mothers, I go gooey. It's the most amazing privilege, but it's totally underrated in our world. Totally underrated. It's the most important thing anybody can do.

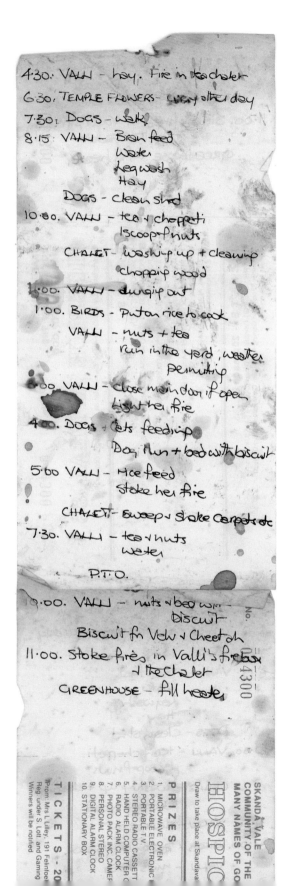

4.30. VALLI - hay. Fire in the chalet
6.30. TEMPLE FLOWERS - every other day
7.30. DOGS - walk
8.15. VALLI - Bran feed
              Water
              Leg wash
              Hay
        DOGS - clean shed
10.30. VALLI - tea + chapati
               1 scoop of nuts
        CHALET - washing up + cleaning
                 chopping wood
11.00. VALLI - dunging out
1.00. BIRDS - put on rice to cook
      VALLI - nuts + tea
              run in the yard, weather
                      permitting
3.00. VALLI - close main door if open
              Light her fire
4.00. DOGS - Cats feeding
             Dog Run + bed with biscuit
5.00. VALLI - rice feed
              Stoke her fire
        CHALET - sweep + shake carpets etc
7.30. VALLI - tea + nuts
              water
        P.T.O.
9.00. VALLI - nuts + bed with
                      Biscuit
        Biscuit for Valli + Cheetah
11.00. Stoke fires in Valli's firebox
                    + the Chalet
        GREENHOUSE - fill heater

SWAMI KARUNA:

I thought Guru was crazy! What do you want to bring an elephant here for? Surely, it would eat us out of house and home.

SWAMI KARUNA: I had to convert the barn for her and about three weeks before Valli was due to arrive, Guru just said, 'Brother Peter, you're looking after the elephant.'

I didn't sleep for two years! I had to boil five gallons of water every four hours, but I had a wood burning stove which only lasted two hours—and it was so small. So yeah...no sleep. I didn't sleep in the bed anyway, I slept in the straw by Valli. But I'd be lucky if I had any straw in the morning because she used to pinch it through the night and I'd just have enough to put under my head.

Dunging out used to take me four hours. Then I'd go and lie in the straw. She'd come over and put her head in my lap to sleep and you'd be lying there for an hour and a half. Your legs would be killing you from this big baby head, but there was immense, immense joy in those times.

LEFT: Swami Karuna's daily routine, from his diary.
RIGHT: Swami with Valli near the Lord Murugan temple.

05. THE DIVINE MOTHER

I was never a believer of Mother. She first had to follow me, by my car—for nearly about three weeks.

JUSTIN: I used to drive Guru up and down the hill in the Land Rover and I remember on one occasion he said, 'Do you see the tiger?'

'Guru, what do you mean tiger? Do you mean squirrel?' 'No, there's a tiger following us, it's huge!' 'Well it's not in the rear-view mirror...'

Next day, same thing—and this went on for about a month. Never Durga, just the tiger. I slightly suspect Durga was testing the waters; sending her vahana first just to see how that was accepted, and if all was well, She might ride it one day and put in an appearance Herself...

146

GURU: I had just finished my prayers and was about to go to sleep. As I relaxed in bed, I could feel somebody coming and sitting next to me. It was a very funny feeling which I could neither rationalise nor understand because I could not see who it was. I plucked up courage and asked myself: 'Who is this who has come and sat on my bed behind me?' As I was thinking this, I could feel that the rhythm of my body had changed. It was like a ripple in the ocean. Every muscle was moving like the waves of the ocean, every muscle in the body was vibrating. 'My goodness!' I thought, 'Some terrible force is trying to enter me!'

Immediately, I called out: 'Who are you?' and as I was saying 'Who are you?' She shifted Her position so She could put a knee in my back. When She did that, my whole body erupted like a volcano. I was literally shaken to the core by the vibrations in my body. Mustering every sinew in my mind that I could so as to retain control, I again called out: 'Who are You?'

In response, I felt the bed being pressed as She got up and came around the bed. Still, though, I hadn't seen Her. All I could see was Her hair, which was like a mass of

tentacles gripping not only me but every part of the room as well, and the more I tried to understand it, the more difficult it was. You just couldn't rationalise in your mind what was happening.

So, with Her hair curling all about me, and now feeling a great deal of apprehension and fear, I once more sought to know who this presence was, adding: 'I would love to see you'. At this, She suddenly turned around and looked at me, and whilst She was looking at me She changed from being someone very old and severe who was both male and female, into the most beautiful lady you could imagine.

She then thrust this amazing head of hair into my face and at that moment everything disintegrated. There was no matter. There was no form. 'I am your Mother.' And then She left.

LEFT: Kali, the 'Dark One.'

147

Every night, She would disintegrate me, reassemble me, reconstitute me. I'd say to Her, 'Mother, I'm a human being! I can't cope with what you're doing!' She would just roar with laughter and say, 'I made you. I will do what I like with you.'

JUSTIN: I could see what was happening to Guru and it wasn't comfortable. There were times when I thought he stopped breathing completely and I was going to have to call an ambulance. Then, finally a breath would come and I'd breathe a sigh of relief.

I wasn't sleeping very well, I was so concerned, but then I started getting these really powerful experiences too. And I knew when She was coming; it was like the sound of... you know the sound before a tube train appears? There is a lot of rushing air being pushed through the tunnel—loud and just that sort of roar? Well, that was one of Her arrival notes. This mass of energy would come roaring and I thought 'Uh oh, here we go.'

JUSTIN: And Guru quite happily allowed himself to be, what he called, sort of a dismembered... shattered into a million pieces, hoping I suppose, that She would reassemble him the right way at the end.

I wasn't happy about that at all. I was quite happy within my own shell, I wasn't ready to disappear and never come back. So I developed a system where if I could wiggle a toe, I thought I could break this chance of being swept off into another dimension!

GURU: I promise you, if it happened to you, you would have nappy change.

The intensity of that manifestation of Mother
during that whole time period around Guru,
was absolutely silly. It was so intense.

SWAMI SURYANANDA: Before it became the Shakti temple
it was Guru's house; he lived upstairs in a small room.
Downstairs was his dining room and where Mother's
gopuram is now—that was a tropical bird house.

So there was a midnight full moon puja every month
in Guru's dining room to the Divine Mother. They were
amazing, they just rocked! I mean, it was all very dramatic
because you'd hear this chanting going on upstairs. And
everybody would be waiting in anticipation downstairs,
then all these bells would start ringing. Amazing
excitement, you could just feel the whole vibration and
energy was just elevating.

Then Swami Karuna would come down the stairs, holding
the aarti, blowing the conch—and then Justin carrying the
murti of Mother. They'd come down the stairs with the murti
of Mother and put Her on the mahabhisekam table. Then
Guru would come down and he was just *black*—he was so
dark—and there'd be this most intense mahabhisekam.

And in one of these pujas I had the most amazing
experience. It was, literally, the experience of thunder
and lightning, in the room. There was this crack of thunder,
and this massive lightning flash from where the shrine was.
And I just went, 'Whoah!' And I looked around and I thought,
'Didn't anyone else see that?'

And accompanied by this was... it was like being in a
rocket ship. The whole energy in me just went 'Wooosh!'
like you were sitting in a rocket ship going off to Mars or
somewhere. And I was absolutely as high as a kite for days
afterwards. That was my first experience of Mother.

LEFT: On Mahasivaratri 1986, a small Kali murti arrived, dubbed 'Little Mum.'
She soon became the focus of midnight pujas and our annual Kali Procession.

We had no idea what to expect.

JUSTIN: And Mr. Singham, a lovely man who ran a temple—the Sri Ganapathy Temple in Wimbledon—he mentioned to Guru that he'd seen a beautiful murti on one of his trips, and thought it would be perfect for Skanda Vale. He told Guru that he wanted to go back and just encourage the sculptor to give the image of Mother more of a smile because it's a very strong image and he didn't want devotees to be frightened.

So the months rolled on and then we got a telephone call saying there was a large box on its way; some haulier was bringing a large box. We met him at the back gate with our old tractor and a very wacky trailer, and returned with this huge crate on the back. We really had quite a lot of fun trying to get it off.

She was just so beautiful.

JUSTIN: Eventually we got it through the door, found a crowbar and pulled off the front of the crate, to see this most beautiful face of this Devi. But we didn't quite know what to do with Her—She was just sort of *there*, in the front room, while all the time Guru thinking 'What to do?' I think he was sort of waiting for a bit of inspiration.

He'd got a lovely menagerie of birds just outside, and he sort of realized that actually that would make a nice spot for Mother, but then what would he do with the birds? He didn't want to move his birds, but thought maybe he'd bring them back into the house.

'No Guru, that is not forward step! We can't have your sitting room as part of some temple with all these birds flying around—imagine you're holding aarti and a parrot flies across? Burnt feathers!' Even so, it took a lot to convince him.

THIS PAGE: Kali moves into Guru's living room.
NEXT PAGE: Guru, Justin and Mr Singham place sacred artefacts to consecrate the foundations of Mother's new temple.

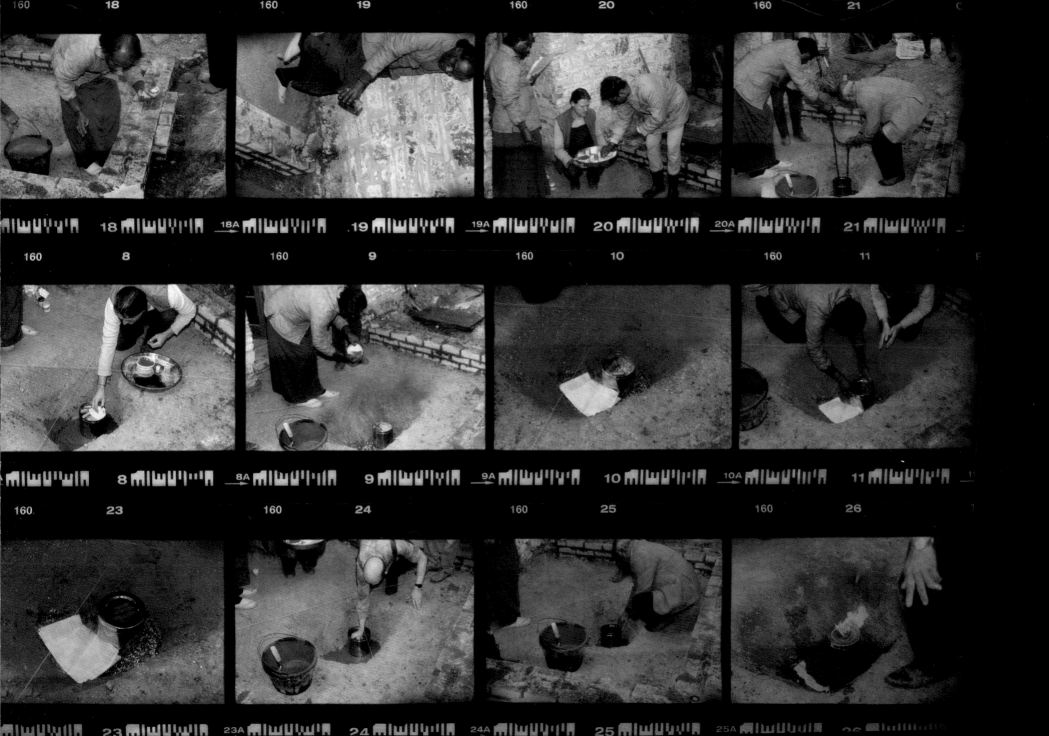

Everything in your life falls into the right perspective.

GURU: If a person has little or no energy, then the possibility of God manifesting is almost impossible. It is just like whipping a dead horse. People might say that they want spirituality, but if they do not conserve their energy and offer it to the Lord or Divine Mother, then the person will not experience the intensity of shakti and power, the grace of God.

In the initial stages, therefore, a bhakta, through his or her devotion, should follow the disciplines of life that help conserve the energy, not dissipate it, so that there is a force, kundalini shakti, with which the Divine Mother can manifest in that person. That is the invitation card. She will then be able to come to you.

You become filled with grace and power. Everything in your life falls into the right perspective. You can't analyse that; it is a feeling that you have. And that feeling you have in the temple is something you want to have again and again, and again. That is what worship is about.

SWAMI SURYANANDA: Mother can come in whatever form She wants to personally manifest to you, but a human needs to first have a power, an inner vitality inside them for Her to use. Then She has something to work with.

Mother is attracted to that power; only then can She manifest something within you. To have energy, it needs to be conserved—mentally, emotionally and physically, otherwise it's like pouring water into a bucket full of holes. The form of the person doesn't matter; it's their purity and vitality which the Divine is attracted to.

You could be a naughty boy, and in a way, we all were naughty boys when we came to Skanda Vale, but there is an essential purity and vitality there which makes you eligible for Mother to work with.

PREVIOUS PAGE: Priests, devotees and community members during the invocation ceremonies.
LEFT: The Maha Shakti Temple opens for public worship.

She has taken over my mind totally. There is no separation any more. She is me and I am Her; it is a continuous interaction.

SWAMI SURYANANDA: Guru was like a child, ecstatic in this experience of Mother manifesting. He loved worshipping Her. Every night, he would lie on the bed and wait for Mother to come. Then he'd go to Little Mum in the shrine, hold Her knee and start talking to Her out loud. He would talk about the Community, the hospice and devotees who needed help. He would ask Her to give people direct experience of Her shakti. Like a child discovering the best thing ever, he longed for people to experience it.'

JUSTIN: You'd ask Guru a question and he'd say, 'Hmm, I'll just have to reflect that with Mother.' It was like a working rapport and it never decreased; it just grew and grew. You realised, after a while, that you weren't talking to Guru any more, but you were really talking to Her.

GURU: The experience of the Divine Mother came about, not because I had superimposed the thought in my mind, but because of our dedication and service to humanity and all of life. She saw how we sought to emulate Franciscan thinking through love, compassion and service to life— providing food and help, counselling and care, and not just to people but for the animals too. The Divine Mother saw what we were doing and Herself manifested to me. She manifested neither in a dream nor in meditation, but truly an experience of Her, physically, and not once but countless times, coming and disintegrating my body, giving me personal shakti, giving me the experience of Her and staying more and more with me.

RIGHT: Guru at the Shakti Temple, during the construction of Mother's gopuram.

06. **SKANDA VALE HOSPICE**

People have this fantasy that a guru is equipped with rubber guts and can eat everything he is given. I used to tell them 'You are killing me!' They really were...

JUSTIN: He had a weakness for cream and rich things. Gilla had baked a black forest gateau with an enormous amount of cream for Greta's birthday and I could see Guru get up to have another slice. 'Guru, you're not really going to have a second slice of that cake, are you?'

'Better to have died having the second slice than to never have had it all!' Then, of course, he gets a heart attack that very night at 3am. 'Oh God', I thought, 'he's had his second slice, and now he's going to die on us.'

I panicked. I was thinking, 'I'm not ready to run this place! He's a guru, he's come with all this power, we're just learning!' I hadn't come with this huge divine inheritance or well, I didn't feel that I had. So, I said, 'Guru, you are not going to die.' We rushed to West Wales General with a bucket between his knees as he was vomiting from the pain. But all he could say was, 'Don't kill the rabbits! You're driving far too fast!' For some reason, that evening there were hundreds and hundreds of rabbits on the road right over to Windy Corner, so I swerved around them all.

And when we arrived there was a stout looking nurse, a wonderful woman, waiting with a wheelchair and as we got out, she started taking his pulse. She had a huge bunch of keys and I could see her running down the corridor, opening a cupboard and coming back with an enormous syringe. I'm not good at syringes, I had to look the other way. I think the timing was just... well, seconds to spare. Anyway, whatever she gave him helped. Guru himself was in another dimension, totally focussed on controlling his heart rate.

RIGHT: Brother James, Brother Ian, Guru and Justin (Swami Shanmukhananda).

JUSTIN: What do you mean you are going for a walk? They are waiting to take you to the mortuary!

GURU: So, they had me on a drip and gave me some injections on a regular basis to stabilise my condition. For four days it was like this and then, on the fifth day, I rose from my bed and sat in a chair. 'Oh, this is quite silly!' I thought. 'This is so ridiculous!'

As I was thinking this, from the fourth-floor window came Mother in the form of a giant bumblebee, and flew straight into me. I instinctively ducked, and as I ducked my whole body suddenly changed, beginning the most amazing revelation.

The next day, when Justin came to see me, I told him that I was going for a walk. 'What do you mean you are going for a walk?' he said, looking more than a little startled. 'They are waiting to take you to the mortuary!' I gave him a big smile. 'That was yesterday!' I said. 'Today is today, and now I am going for a walk!'

Rather than arguing the point, the nurse gave Justin an emergency beeper and, with strict instructions that we should only go just around the corner and back, we went for my walk. I, instead, took him down all the corridors of the hospital.

'Why are you so headstrong?' Justin said, exasperated.

'I am on my sea trials!' I told him. 'I have to be on my feet soon because Mother's full moon puja is in a few days time, and I am going to be there!'

And that is exactly what happened. I came home and I never forget this. Mother's puja was later that night and Justin wanted me to be tucked up in bed upstairs whilst a picture of mine would be placed on a chair in my stead. I was having none of it. I wanted to be at the puja.

'Alright!' he finally conceded. 'But I will conduct the puja, and you will sit on the chair.'

'No way!' I countered. 'I am back, and back in the saddle! I am doing the puja and you can sit on the chair!'

GURU: Since that time, I have not stopped and now I am on a new high. When you have a sense of dedication and a purpose in life, you cannot stop. I am not a minimalist. I dislike it. I live one hundred percent. When everybody has finally gone to bed, I then get up and start my own puja. This might be at two o'clock in the morning, but I carry on with all my activities with Mother. That is my discipline, and more than that, it is my love of God.

LEFT: Guru giving blessings at Guru Purnima, two weeks after his near-fatal heart attack.

JUSTIN: While he was in intensive care, he was much more concerned with somebody next to him who also had a heart attack, who was not doing well at all and was actually slipping away. And it really troubled him that the nurses did what they could, but they hadn't time to sit for hours holding his hand.

Guru could see this man was just terrified—no close family coming and no-one to hold his hand. Guru couldn't do it, he couldn't get out of bed. I remember him talking about it; he said, we have to find a better way for people when they're coming to the end of life; not to die in fear and pain. Okay, the pain could be controlled with morphine, but it was the fear that troubled Guru. Fear was not helpful; we should be surrounded by love and warmth.

I mean, birth is traumatic, but everyone's there. There's nothing nicer than for a young mother to be with her mum and her best friends—and death should be the same thing. It was so clear in his mind, and he never really understood why that service didn't exist and it wasn't happening already. This was really the start of what has now become Skanda Vale Hospice.

PLEASE SUPPORT
THE VALE
HOSPICE APPEAL

LEFT: David Newman raising funds and awareness about the new hospice.
ABOVE: An annual fête opens the temple and hospice to the wider community.

I often think to myself that I belong to the wilds really, not here in civilisation.

GURU: To be the instrument of the Divine Mother is a very daunting experience. People will never understand what it is like to carry such a power in your body and mind. My whole body ripples like the ocean, like the sun. The energy level is so high you can no longer control your faculties. Your mind is not your own, your body is not your own, nor your senses. Even if you were to use your senses it would be on a very superficial level; all your faculties are about the Nature of God. That is what total surrender means, learning to accommodate the vast power and grace of God.

The only thing I do, to earth myself, is to behave like a clown. If I didn't, people would say, 'He's like a saint!' That would put me off immediately. It would be totally unacceptable because I wouldn't then be able to relate to people. On the contrary, I want to be like them. That is what the Lord asked me to do. That is why the Lord sent me to all parts of the world, meeting all kinds of people, living with them, working together with them, so that I could relate to them and they could relate to God.

It was not always easy. This time, God didn't want me to be some rare specimen of humanity meditating in a cave.

RIGHT: In 1990, Guru was invited to lead a spiritual seminar, first at a devotees house and soon after at a larger property in the Swiss alpine village of Kiental. A dedicated community of devotees began to form.

I love the people of Switzerland.

GURU: Yes, people may look at the Swiss and see only the glamorous, affluent side, but I have seen the other side too; the basic farmer who is a simple person. If you go to the mountains, you will find the simple folk: the artisans, the carvers, the builders and merchants—lovely people.

SISTER SASKIA: When he was in Kiental, he was very much amongst the people. We'd have a seminar, have some coffee, have another seminar, then have lunch together. Guru would cook us these incredible feasts! And we always had one day where we went out in the mountains with him. It was beautiful. And he had such a wicked sense of humour. Absolutely wicked! I mean, he could really manage all those people. He was on stage, no? He was in his element.

SISTER MARIA: For me, that was one of the most important things: when somebody teaches something, to see how it is living in that person. What are the fruits of all that teaching? And that was no question with Guru. He was not a preacher or someone who reads a lot of books, so I think they could see that he was really living these values.

As soon as somebody came into contact with Guru, there was so much love. He was just like a walking love! This feeling which came out of him was so strong; this love, this joy, this humour. Oh, everybody was so inspired by that.

LEFT: A day spent hiking in the mountains was a regular feature of the Kiental seminar program.

In the silence of your own thoughts you will discover God.

GURU: You must begin to listen. Go to the mountains, quietly. Spend time there; put up a tent in the night by yourself, sit quietly and listen. Sit and listen to the vast space and energy that comes from the universe throughout the entire mountain range; that is the energy.

If you sit down and begin to meditate, you can draw that energy into your whole being and merge with it—it will revitalise you completely. By listening to that sound, you move away from the world of vibrations, and enter in the consciousness of Divine energy.

RIGHT: In 1995, the Swiss community bought this mountain lodge near the village of Fideris in Graubünden, as a permanent place to hold seminars and, one day, to develop it into a temple.

08. LORD MURUGAN TEMPLE

relationship with the Lord and He will destroy all that impairs your progress spiritually. He is the Commander-in-Chief of the three worlds; in the vastness of the empire of the whole universe, he steps out from a million suns. He wants to identify Himself with you and give you security and love. Call on the Lord. Share with the Lord. He will teach you how to be exact in your life and be very well disciplined. To worship Lord Subramanium is a very disciplined act of worship.

SWAMI NARAYANA: The Murugan Temple expanded bit by bit over the years. Then, after the Shakti temple was completed, Guru decided that it was time for it to be totally revamped. So we started on the extension—the back part of the temple. We were digging these enormous footings; a metre deep by a metre wide, then mixing the concrete by hand with wheelbarrows and shovels.

At a certain point I said to Guru, 'Well, what should we do now? And he said 'Nothing.' So I said, 'Okay.' I was learning my lesson by then—if I was told something, I'd just shut up—and so nothing happened.

Then, after about a week, this truck pulled up outside the site and unloaded hundreds of blocks—just delivered like that, without being ordered. A devotee had decided to donate a big pile of blocks, and Guru said, 'Well, now you can start.' So that's what I did; we built the walls and so on, and it went from there. Then, a close devotee opened an account for us with Jewsons builders merchant, and said 'This is for the temple, you just order what you want,' extraordinary generosity—a blank cheque.

SWAMI GOVINDA: Tight up against the eastern side of the proposed build was a eucalyptus tree. We wanted to align the new temple extension with the original farmhouse, but this would mean chopping the tree down. Guru wouldn't let anyone touch that tree—so if you look closely, you'll see that the extension is off-centre from the original farmhouse. By the same measure, on the western side of the project there were several beautiful shrubs and the remains of an old hedgerow; again we had to carefully dig around these plants when building. The temple extension was carefully built between these life forms.

SWAMI GOVINDA: Every day on the site we would get a visit from Guru; he would quietly walk around, 'minding his own business,' as he would say, but quietly energising us and the work—energising and bringing Shakti to the raw fabric of this temple.

LEFT: Guru outside the Lord Murugan Temple.
NEXT PAGE: Blessing the foundations of the temple extension.

It was the first time in the history of Skanda Vale that we weren't squirreling around for materials. Pallets of cement arrived, a whole truckload of blocks, virgin timber with no rusty nails buried in it—it really was a new era.

SWAMI GOVINDA: On one of my chaotic early visits to Skanda Vale, I heard Guru saying, 'When the Murugan temple is complete my work is over.' I took this to mean he wouldn't be with us much longer.

Somewhere in the depths of my mind I grasped that I needed to get down there, at least for a while. By the time I arrived, the footings had just been completed but nothing more. My first weeks were spent endlessly digging alongside Swami Narayana. Followed by non-stop concreting; all mixed on the back of a tractor, then carted over and levelled by hand. Seriously back-breaking work. But every day was exciting, every day I found myself charging into the work, fired up to push the project along. You have no idea the depth of pleasure and deep fulfilment that I got from swinging a pickaxe, shovelling soil and pushing a wheelbarrow.

Each stage of the build was a revelation; this was the first time I had brought a building out of the ground and I was so keen to learn and absorb every aspect of its detail. From foundations to walls, to roof structure and slates, then render and plaster, doors and windows. I was obsessed, tearing myself away from work just before nine at night, and not at all if I could get away with it.

The extension took just over a year, and in the same time I understood, crystal clear, that this is where I belong and need to stay. Needless to say, Guru actually lived for another 15 years.

The Lord was very specific: 'I want pillars in black and gold marble to support My temple.'

GURU: We travelled to Carrara in Tuscany, Italy. It was a very hot day and the proprietor walked us round and around, showing us stack after stack of cut and uncut marble before finally taking us back to his office. 'Now, Guru, can you tell me what you have decided?' he asked.

'You are going to be very disappointed because the Lord does not want any of what you have shown me.' I replied. He sighed, wearily. 'Then what do you want?' 'The Lord wants black and gold marble.' At this, he clasped his head with both hands; 'But there is only one such seam, and I just don't have any!'

'I will tell you what we will do,' I said. 'We will have lunch, and in the meantime, I will ask the Lord to help you find the marble we need.'

We left his office and returned to the hotel, whereupon I sat down on my bed and, looking out at the sea, began praying to the Lord. 'Lord,' I said, 'You are the ocean. You have given me a task to find black and gold marble for Your temple,' and I asked Him for His help.

You have no idea; we arrived at his office after lunch to find the happiest man in the world. 'Guru, I have got the marble for you!' he exclaimed triumphantly, and took us to where he had stored the block of marble stone, so we could see for ourselves.

People don't realise that, when you are working with God, everything is available. Everything is available! We had it shipped back and began putting it up.

190

Lord Subramanium is born of the energy of
Lord Siva. That energy is so powerful that
He can destroy anything, any evil force.

SWAMI SURYANANDA: What was unique about the Lord Murugan Temple was that we were developing a new physical structure on top of an incredibly powerful existing temple. Guru explained to me that the Lord had been manifesting in that particular place, intensely, for a long period of time. So the power and energy of God was connected to that physical space and disturbing it would have destructive consequences. It was only possible because he was there.

Guru was very, very tense. I remember him saying that whilst these foundations were open (before all the sacred items, murtis and relics were sealed in concrete) that negative forces could try get in to manipulate the existing and future power of the temple. Power attracts power; positive energy attracts negative energies. And so, Guru talked about having to encircle the whole of that area with fire to protect it; to keep out any adharmic forces whilst the physical building work was going on.

One thing I remember well was when Guru was offering the aarti in front of the place of where Lord Siva was going to be installed. You could feel him literally bring the energy of Siva to be sealed into that physical space. It was absolutely phenomenal, just watching Guru's face and his whole being, bringing that energy of Siva.

He did the same with the five niches of Ganesha, Lakshmi, Vishnu, Sarasvati and Siva, each was physically linked to the gopuram with holy thread, forming a yantra. The inspiration and details on how to do all of this came straight from the Divine. There was no studying; Guru just followed the instructions of the Lord, step by step, in whatever he did.

LEFT: Blessing the temple foundations. Guru said that knowledge from the Agama Sastras—ancient texts detailing the esoteric science of temple building—were revealed to him for this consecration.

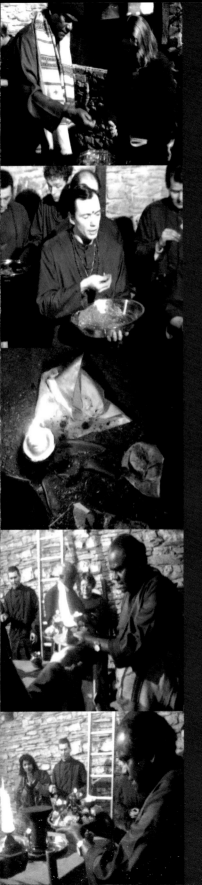

193

LEFT: Lord Shanmukha moves from his temporary home to the new gopuram. **RIGHT:** Guru with the murti of Subramanium from Badulla.

RIGHT: The new temple inauguration.

The real temple is there in your heart.

GURU: There is no purpose in just having a temple. The temple of the heart and the temple of action go together. The temple of action is to serve God. That is the temple. If you have no love, how on earth can you know God? You have no space and time for God. Your ego is so wrapped up in yourself that there is no space and time for God.

Love is the hallmark of spirituality. Love is God. God is love. It is not a cliché. It must be pulsating in your veins. It cannot be clinical. Obedience is absolute. Because of that absolute obedience to God, God has taken me over lock, stock and barrel in my mind and body. I function because of the Lord. I live because of the Lord. I drink and eat because of the Lord, for the inspiration is the energy of God, telling me how to make Skanda Vale's service to humanity even better, and providing all the resources. My confidence in God is the development of the mind and the surrender of the human being—total and absolute surrender.

LEFT: Lord Subramanium, Valli and Devani at the culmination of the temple inauguration.

09. **SRI RANGANATHA TEMPLE**

I'm under the stars, on the ocean of infinity.

SWAMI SURYANANDA: Straight after Mother's mahabhisekam, we were all having dinner and Guru came in fizzing with excitement: 'Listen, listen! The Lord has just shown me the most incredible temple for us to build for Lord Ranganatha!'

We huddled around the table to listen. He was enthralled; he explained to us how rare it was that a temple was directly ordained by the Lord, and with such specific instructions. The first two temples were too, of course, but they both essentially started out as living rooms—even the shrine in Earl's Court was just a bedroom. What Lord Vishnu had instructed was on another scale entirely: a huge rock wall dug into the field, a series of lakes, the entire structure open to the elements.

GURU: Lord Vishnu opened the screen of my mind and pointed to the land where the cattle were grazing, saying, 'I want you to build a temple there.'

He said, 'I want you to build two lakes, and I shall be lying in the ocean. I have no roof and everything must be open. I want you to give people an opportunity to come and worship Me there at any time. Bring all the religions into it, because all faiths are embodied in Me. I am religion. I am Sanatana Dharma, the timeless consciousness of Me. All this, I want you to build.'

When He said that, I told Him: 'My Lord, I don't know what to do. There are cattle grazing there!'

'I will give you more land very soon,' He replied, and within a fortnight that is exactly what happened; we were given some land.

LEFT: Sri Ranganatha with the serpent Adishesha, Lakshmi and Brahma.

I will provide you with all that you need.

GURU: One important task was to look for murtis identical to what I had seen, so I began ringing up various people. It so happened that around this time, I had a bhajan meeting to attend in London and when I arrived, I saw that Mr Singham was there. After the meeting was over, I sat down in my chair and he came and sat at my feet. 'Guruji, what can I do for you?' he asked, so I told him. 'I want to go to India, Mr. Singham.' At this, he started to laugh. 'And why do you want to go to India?'

'I am looking for images of Sri Ranganatha, Lakshmi, Hanuman and Brahma suitable for a temple we are about to construct.'

'But I have got them already!' I looked at him greatly surprised. 'How can this be? I have only just told you this!'

'I know!' he replied, beaming broadly. 'But I was in India recently and happened to come across the very same images you have described. I thought I should buy them. They will be arriving in about three or four weeks!'

RIGHT: The murtis arrive. **NEXT PAGE:** They are smeared with kumkum and sandalwood paste, ready for their consecration.

202

The monks built it.

GURU: And so, we set about structuring every single thing—digging lakes, building the containers for vast amounts of water that flowed from the hillside.

We didn't pay anybody to do anything. The monks built it all. They worked very hard. Swami Suryananda and Swami Brahmananda on two tractors and diggers at two or three o'clock in the morning—when I arrived, they were like *that*... [mimics]. So tired! People worked very, very hard.

SWAMI SURYANANDA: I got up at six o'clock in the morning and was on the digger until about ten o'clock at night, then I had some food and went to bed. That was it, every single day, for nine months.

I remember being amazed at how my own capacity was extended. If I wasn't on the digger, or fixing reinforcement, or moving rocks, or making cement, I was on the computer, doing orders, on the telephone, doing research, paying bills. It was absolutely non stop. Not even five minutes break. I was watching myself thinking 'how is this happening?'

I was given the grace to do that work.

SWAMI NARAYANA: Guru used to say, 'nobody changes unless their back is to the wall.' So he would push and push, until our back was to the wall, and then there'd be some change. That's what it was all about; change, evolution—being shown that you do have the capacity to draw upon divine energy—you do, everybody has that, but you need a situation which demands it.

SWAMI GOVINDA: If anyone had told us at the beginning that we were going to build that kind of temple in that amount of time, we would have said, 'Forget it. No way. Never going to happen.' But Guru made us realise first-hand what you can achieve when you work with the Divine.

RIGHT: Swami Suryananda and Markus take a four-and-a-half minute break.

Nobody changes unless their back is to the wall.

SWAMI NARAYANA: You just had to be absolutely, totally flexible. We were taught that. That was a big, big lesson in being one with God—that you just have to surrender. It comes to a point where everything, every minute of your day, every ounce of your energy is being directed by the Lord to do something. By the fact that you just agreed within yourself to do everything, to do anything.

I suppose that's actually the essence of bhakti yoga—it's not so much about the ecstasy of an experience but just that total surrender. So there's nothing, you're empty, nothing there. There's just this automaton, doing things for the Lord. You become one with an energy which is overriding individual consideration. There's no individual consideration—not there.

208   **RIGHT**: Swami Narayana on the boulder wall behind Sri Ranganatha.

That rock is in the wrong place.

SWAMI NARAYANA: We were halfway through building the wall at the back, behind the lake. There was a point where we had to move things by hand. So we had a rolling gantry and there was this huge rock which we put where Lord Siva is now. It took two days to move something like ten meters.

And after two days, around midnight, we were standing around, sort of congratulating ourselves, agreeing what a wonderful rock it was, and we heard this rumble of Guru's Land Rover. He got out rather slowly and said, 'Mother sent me down to tell you that rock is in the wrong place. Get it out of there.' And he got back into the Land Rover and disappeared again!

But such is our level of surrender at that point there was no hesitation. Nobody said, 'oh, well, we can't do that, we've spent two days moving it.' They said, 'okay, we'll move it.' You know, there was just an acceptance that the Divine was directing that operation.

LEFT: Cleaning the rock for Sri Ranganatha to lie on.

We simply worked around the clock.

SWAMI YOGANANDA: The entire last week I slept two hours a night. And then I didn't sleep the last night. I came to a state where I literally couldn't lay paving anymore, because my brain couldn't put patterns together. And I could fall asleep pushing a wheelbarrow full of sand; you only wake up when you fall over. There's nothing you can do; you can try and run and you still fall asleep.

Once you go to that degree, you get in a state of mind where you are beyond pressure. There comes a state where your mind hasn't got the power to worry or be annoyed— it's just quiet because it's too exhausted. Trance is not quite the right word, but the mind becomes really even. You just act, and you were too tired to have an opinion on it.

You only realize just how much you're able to do when you have somebody like Guru pushing you along.

214   **RIGHT:** Carefully lowering the murti of Sri Ranganatha.

I think you've all conveniently forgotten...

SWAMI SURYANANDA: We'd been working absolutely flat out, all the members of the Community and this big team of devotees going day and night, literally. As we got closer to the inauguration, the normal time frame went out the window. Everyone started to panic because we're not going to get this ready on time, and you've really got to go for it.

Then Guru came up to us and said, I think you've all conveniently forgotten about the lake, the big lake. And we thought, 'Oh God.' Because we had conveniently forgotten about this third lake, Mother's Lake, because we just thought no way are we going to even remotely start that.

And Guru said 'It's going to happen, you're going to start it now and it will be ready in time.' That was three weeks before the inauguration.

RIGHT: A large group of ladies worked around the clock in heavy rain to shovel sand and roll out a large pond liner so that the Durga Lake would be ready in time for the inauguration.

Narayana is in every single thing. You are a part of Narayana. You are God yourself.

SWAMI SURYANANDA: The energy that we carried during this time was phenomenal. Even though we didn't go to a single puja, we were just energized with this shakti, this focus, purpose and grace.

Guru didn't say, 'Oh, this has to go here. This has to go there.' But you knew that inspiration was coming through you; how to do things, how to move things, what to order. So he was absolutely active but playing this role of 'Why are you asking me? Go and ask Mother. I don't know a thing.'

He would use those projects to make you make that effort. It's an easy option; 'Oh Guru, what do we do now? Where do we dig a hole? What do we put in here?' And in the early days he would say, but then as time went on, he absolutely wouldn't say. He would actually get very angry if you asked him. That was a clear change in how Skanda Vale operated, from when I first came.

It was one of the most beautiful things that Guru gave to us—pushing us into that orbit of direct personal experience of God. Showing you that it works, through experience.

He said, 'My job is to teach you the highest yoga, which is living in the world, but not being part of it. That's my job, so that you're able to fully experience and express your karma, yet remain centered in the Divine.' He said, 'People can spend years and years meditating in the cave to come out, and then get swallowed by the world.'

He wanted you to be natural, be normal, express yourself, yet have the ability to withdraw and center yourself in the energy of God. There isn't any aspect of living that God isn't part of, and that was what Guru was trying to show us: that God is in everything.

I would regard the building of Lord Vishnu's temple as the most important part of my life. That is my epitaph. There is nothing more.

10. RIGHTS OF WAY

How dare someone obstruct the right for people to come and worship here.

A new drama began when local companies started overcharging for minibus transfers to Skanda Vale.

Guru would not tolerate pilgrims being ripped off, so initiated the building of a coach park so pilgrims could travel directly to Skanda Vale without minibus transfers.

One neighbour wasn't happy...

SWAMI SURYANANDA: The neighbour lived on the track near the coach park entrance. It was the same track we had used to come in and out of Skanda Vale for 25 years, but he grew very irate about more people passing through, despite there being only one or two coaches a week. He suddenly claimed that he owned the track and that we didn't have any right of way over it. He then threatened to stop any traffic coming into Skanda Vale.

Guru's reaction was strong—it seemed disproportionate at the time. In my mind, I was thinking, 'why can't we just have a chat with the guy, I'm sure we can resolve it?' But Guru was ranting and raving that this person was trying to stop people coming to worship God and that we would fight it tooth and nail.

SWAMI GOVINDA: It's another example of what I call 'Guru logic.' Something which, at the time, makes no sense to us whatsoever. But Guru sees the bigger picture.

Tomorrow morning, get in the JCB and bulldoze the trailer out the way. No one is stopping anyone from coming to Skanda Vale.

SWAMI SURYANANDA: The neighbour had parked his pickup and trailer across the entrance. No one could leave or enter, so we called the police, but they couldn't make him move as this was a civil dispute that had to be settled in court.

Guru was at a seminar in Switzerland, so I phoned him up and he said 'tomorrow morning, get in the JCB and bulldoze the trailer out the way. No one is stopping anyone from coming to Skanda Vale.' His language was much more colourful than that, but you get the idea.

I had this drama going on in my mind 'What do I do? Do I actually get in the JCB, bulldoze this trailer and potentially get arrested for property damage, or provoke physical confrontation?' It wasn't something I was looking forward to, but Guru was extremely clear. He would never incite violence of any kind but in my mind, the night before, I said 'Okay. I'm going to do it. This is what obedience to Guru is about. Obedience to the Divine. Just trust implicitly that it's the right thing to do.'

Then, funnily enough, the next morning, Guru rang up literally seconds after the 5am puja saying, 'Mother's directed a change of plan. Contact the solicitors, find a barrister and seek a legal injunction to prevent him blocking the track.'

The Lord does not send faint-hearted people
to do this work. You must always be connected,
your solutions always found by the Divine.
Non-violence—that is the only way.

GURU: Last night, before bed, I had a chat with Mother and explained the situation very clearly. See, when you talk to the Divine, you must never exaggerate. Absolute truth. Absolute honesty. And you will get an absolute response from Her very, very quickly. I said, 'Mother, what are we to do? This is Your will. We serve you.' She became so amused, She always does! And Her solution was absolutely amazing, She said:

It's very simple. Tell all the Community members and the pilgrims at the Sunday puja to greet you at the place where the neighbours do not want you to go. Tell them to come with drums, come with conches, come with flowers, everything, and follow your motorhome in procession down the track. And if he stops you, do not say anything. Stop the vehicle. Park it nicely. And there, do a puja. The police will be told that we are doing a puja and the roads will be blocked by the pilgrims. Simple.

Extracts from Guru's Kiental seminar, Switzerland, March 2006.

On the day of the procession the elements unleashed across the valley. In torrential rain and gale-force winds, devotees gathered to welcome Guru home.

SWAMI GOVINDA: Guru would often take two murtis with him to Swiss seminars, usually Mother and Lord Shanmukha. I remember helping him pack before that particular trip and he picked up Lord Murugan—the murti we call 'Battle Murugan.' Guru saw me look at him quizzically and said, 'This one needs to come this time.'

RIGHT: Battle Murugan.

SWAMI SURYANANDA: It really felt like one of these ancient battles from the time of Rama or Krishna. Everything felt heightened, surreal almost, with the moon in the sky, the mist, the wind and rain. We made a battle chariot—a tractor trailer with loads of lights and a drum machine on the back. So, when we started in procession, singing bhajans to Murugan, with the rain slashing down and all these young devotees shouting 'Arohara! Arohara!' it really did feel like we were marching into battle.

Then, as we got close to the neighbour's house, all the conches blew, the bhajans got louder, the lights on the chariot came on, and the drum machines started full blast. You can imagine the sheer noise and energy! The atmosphere was electric. A hundred voices chanting and singing, aartis blowing about in the wind. Then, the neighbour came out cursing and twirling this shepherd's crook around his head.

SISTER CAROL: I said to him, 'What on earth is all of this for? All this anger and hatred. You have threatened us, deceived us, blocked us and because of what? Because we worship God? Because other people come here to worship God?'

SWAMI SURYANANDA: I remember seeing the headlights on Guru's motorhome shining through the mist. And he was standing there, holding this murti of Lord Subramanium out in front of him. And as he presented the Lord, these young lads bounced the neighbour's pickup out of the way and pushed the trailer into the verge. It was loaded with heavy slates and they literally bounced it out the way.

Then Guru drove down the track, followed by the chariot and the procession behind him. I was busy getting a verbal caution from the police as the 'instigator' of the procession, but from that moment the track was never blocked again.

I am a thug, with the nature of a saint.

GURU: Divine friends, I have no intention ever of bowing to the will of ignorant people. I was sent by the Lord to establish dharma and the will of the Divine must prevail. This was not a victory over anybody; this is a victory over stupidity, arrogance, envy, hatred—over the viciousness of a human being. A very, very silly person who is filled with tremendous anger. You have no idea how many obstacles this person has created; stirring the Council to object to us being here.

He cannot stir anything because I know well in advance what is happening. When I say that not one leaf falls from the tree without Mother knowing, don't you think that Her son knows it too? Divine friends, you will never, ever be alone when you are with God—that partnership with God is what Skanda Vale is about.

This is your temple, this is your place of worship. So, always be convinced to do the right thing. I have not asked you to cause harm to anybody or to break the law, but if a person violates the law of karma, they will suffer the consequences of those actions. I am a General of God. You are His army. Today you did what was necessary to remove the obstacles to liberation.

THIS PAGE: Transcript and video stills from Guru's talk.

236

A time will come when I die. The members of the Swami's Council will get together and take on the responsibility of maintaining that link and conviction in the Lord. Intensity of worship is their anchor for spirituality.

SWAMI SURYANANDA: I was the main witness for Skanda Vale at the High Court hearing. I'd lived this whole case every single day for a year so I knew it absolutely inside out. It was quite an amazing experience when I was called to the stand because I felt this satyam, this truth just flowing through me. You could hear a pin drop in the Court. There was the most phenomenal vibration in there.

The opposing case just fell apart. The Judge had visited Skanda Vale as part of the hearing and he was categorically clear that Skanda Vale was not only a place of worship, it was also an ashram, a monastery, a sanctuary for life. He issued a High Court Ruling which legitimised access not only for coaches and cars, but for tractors, trailers, fuel tankers. We won the case convincingly.

SWAMI GOVINDA: That's the 'Guru logic' because ultimately, you realise that this entire drama was brought about by Guru and the Divine to give us this High Court Ruling. And that High Court Ruling was a leap forward in the development of Skanda Vale. It embedded Skanda Vale in the law of the land, putting us in a much stronger position for the future, especially in our relationship with the local planning authorities.

Prior to that, they had tried to deal with us as a farmstead with places of worship 'on it,' ignoring the fact that tens of thousands of people were coming here every year to worship and serve and pray. So, the High Court Ruling was pivotal for everything we would do next.

SWAMI SURYANANDA: From the day of that judgement, I got this really clear feeling that Guru was now hands-off. Like he was saying, 'That's me done now. I hand over all practical responsibility to the Swami's Council and Community members.' Guru had spent an entire year gradually removing himself from the meetings, removing himself from finance, and eventually removing himself from the whole running of Skanda Vale.

LEFT: A painting of the murtis of Lord Shanmukha, Valli and Devani from the Murugan Temple.

239

11. GURU'S SAMADHI

SWAMI GOVINDA: It would have been in about 2006 that Guru started getting ill. He had serious amount of fluid on his lungs—so the doctor proposed to insert a small needle into his back and drain the lungs over a few days. Guru looked at him and said, 'In two days time I have to go to Switzerland and give a seminar.' The doctor looked at him and said, 'I'm really sorry but…'

Guru was adament; 'You don't understand. I'm going to Switzerland and you have to make sure this liquid is off my lungs before I go.' So, the doctor conceded, and ended up performing what we knew to be quite a dangerous procedure, pushing this massive needle through Guru's back, between his ribs and into the lungs. You could literally see this water pouring out into a bottle. It was extremely painful, but two days later, Guru went to Switzerland and held the seminar.

A few months later, his health had worsened but he'd got used to managing it, and he was now on oxygen. I just remember him before going to Switzerland again; I was

holding him, and he put his hand on the banister, took the first step—he was breathing really heavily—and he just said one word: 'Resolute.'

He could just about get the word out, he was so short of breath. He was so ill. And I just thought, this is the last time I'm going to see you. You're not going to come back. He actually did the seminar, with an oxygen bottle, and he did a lot of it out on the mountainside, because he wasn't getting enough air into his lungs.

When he got back, we arranged a whole day of medical examinations, specialised scans and appointments with different consultants. But the night before all this was due to take place, Guru discharged himself from hospital.

Slowly, it began to dawn on us that Guru was not going to get any better.

LEFT: The September 2006 seminar was Guru's last visit to Switzerland. Six months later, he moved to Skanda Vale Hospice for 24 hour care.

One time I was with him when he was very ill he said, 'I love to suffer because I love God.'

SWAMI GOVINDA: Most people tend to assume that the karma which a Master takes on can only manifest physically. But karma can manifest mentally, emotionally, even spiritually. And that's not easy to witness; seeing this great Master, this limitless, powerful being who you look to for all your strength, to suddenly depend on you completely. To feed him, to dress him, to lift his head, to do everything for him.

In one moment, he would exude this almost awe-inspiring intensity of Yogeshwara, and in the next moment, he was a dependent and elderly person. So, we were just doing our best to keep responding day to day. We were obviously very privileged to do that for him, but at the time, it was very raw. It was like no other challenge we had been through. We were dealing with a real, human feeling of uncertainty.

SWAMI SURYANANDA: I remember, people were trying to make sense of what was happening to Guru—trying to understand it. And during that period, I used to go to the Sri Ranganatha Temple to do my own puja every night. And one time I had a revelation; the Lord said, 'People think that the manifestation of karma is physical suffering. But it's physical, emotional, psychological and spiritual. Karma manifests throughout the whole being and that is what is happening to Guru.'

Anything that he could possibly do to serve the divinity in another life, he would do. He would use his whole being to the maximum extent to enable that other life to realise God. It was profoundly beautiful and simple.

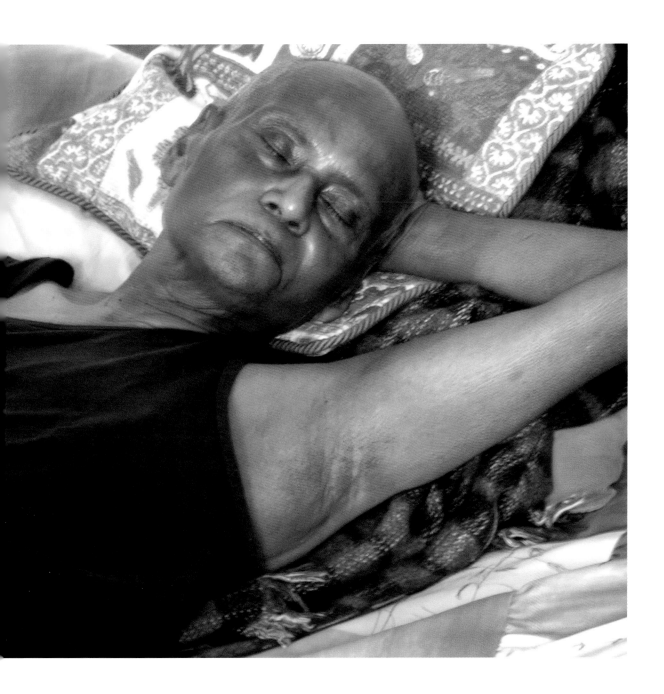

SWAMI NARAYANA: We all knew that Guru was taking karma on, although he wouldn't talk about it very much. I remember one time, we had a dog called Penny, a lurcher, and she was out in the yard when something happened with her. I don't know if she dislocated her leg or had an accident or something, but this dog screamed and screamed, and then suddenly stopped.

I ran into the house to tell Guru that something was wrong with Penny, and as I came up the stairs, Justin told me Guru had just deliberately slammed his arm in the door of this big cast iron safe. And that was the precise point when Penny's screaming stopped.

LEFT: Guru at Skanda Vale Hospice.

SWAMI GOVINDA: In those last few weeks, Guru's energy had expanded so much. It was like he enveloped everything. And you could feel it in Skanda Vale; his energy was so abundant, so tangible, you could almost grab it by the armful. In his room at the hospice, the vibration was like a temple. Of course, we were still caring for someone with human needs, but we were so wrapped up in this warmth and grace, just soaking in that energy.

Then one morning, we had a strong feeling that the whole Community should come over to see Guru as soon as possible. Everyone had the opportunity to quietly spend time in Guru's presence and pay their final respects. Some hadn't seen Guru for a long time and found it very difficult to see him like that. It was actually pretty raw.

In contrast, Guru's death itself was the lightest, sweetest transition you could possibly imagine. Like a tiny bubble bursting, incredibly delicate and light.

SWAMI SURYANANDA: He had talked about this vintage Armagnac for over twenty years to everyone in the Community. It was such a strong wish of his; 'You must all sit down together and drink it on my behalf!' It had become this slightly mythical thing at the back of a dark cupboard. And that evening, we actually almost forgot about it until someone said, 'Wait, the Armagnac!' So, we gathered, toasted his life and enjoyed this most exquisite drink, just as he had wished.

SWAMI GOVINDA: We all knew for over two decades where Guru wanted to be buried, a very special place towards the Shakti temple alongside the deer on the edge of woodland. He wanted to be encased in tons of concrete to protect and preserve the power that lay within him. He always said angels would be seen there—whether he meant mortal angels or heavenly was not for us to know.

RIGHT: Bucketloads of flower petals were offered.

246

SWAMI AMBA: Guru's corpse was in a sacred space in the marquee opposite the samadhi, I was on 'guard duty' from 01:30–03:30. Like everybody I was exhausted and stressed. I tried to deny, rationalise and dismiss the vibration I felt emanating from Guru's body. It was wave after wave of pure, impersonal, universal love.

Late that morning I was a pall bearer of the coffin. As we entered the samadhi site, the incline and mud made the opposite bearer lose control and the coffin cut into my shoulder, taking a huge amount of the weight. I thought 'Guru, you're crushing me even in death!'

At this moment I felt Guru by my side laughing hysterically at my predicament. As we placed the coffin down, the funeral director was clearly annoyed at many of the monks laughing. 'Boys,' he said, 'the Guru is dead and this is his funeral.'

SWAMI ISHWARANANDA: Guru didn't die. Yes, we buried a body which he and the Divine had animated for 70-something years, covered it with tons of concrete and a beautiful rock, but that was just the shell of the Guru. Was I sad? It was my birthday, how could I be sad? I felt he knew I would like the idea, though of course untrue, that he couldn't tell me off any more. You can't bury a Guru.

SISTER FRANCESCA: Guru was no more. It had been a very strange week in the ashram following Guruji's demise. Monks and nuns going about their daily chores, united and separated in their individual grief not able to share their experience in the most meaningful way; through the pouring out of their hearts to God in collective worship because the temples were closed for a week.

Our Guru had taken maha samadhi. We could pay our respects in the marquee at the top of the hill where his body lay in state. The colour of eternity itself. I think I had only seen Guruji's skin so very dark, blending with the colour of the cosmos itself, on the day as a frightened young novice I took my monastic vows. This was no man in front of me. Then or now. It was truly the Divine inhabiting a human body.

I tried somehow to say thanks to Him. Once again in my life, surely not for the first time, knowing me inside out, yet still willing to take on the massive task of guiding me towards God. But mine was a poor effort compared to what had happened months earlier, the day before he left Skanda Vale to take up residence at the Hospice. I was on Mother's Temple terrace, arranging flowers as usual and a stumbling Guru entered the terrace on his own, barely able to walk. He softly uttered 'Thank you' and was gone. His love beyond measure, beyond comprehension.

　　RIGHT: Devotees in procession to Guru's Samadhi.

12. SHAMBO

He warned us; 'As I approach my death, I will really give you a run for your money. I will go out with such a bang.' We just thought, 'Oh God, it's bad enough as it is!'

In 2007, Skanda Vale was at the centre of an intense political debate about the sanctity of life. Curiously, the events that played out synchronised perfectly with the key stages of Guru's final illness and death...

SWAMI SURYANANDA: They could arrive here at any point in time and try and kill Shambo. The fact is that during the period between now and when our solicitors are able to apply for a High Court injunction to prevent the slaughter, we are very vulnerable and so it's very important that we resist any attempt to kill him. The best way of doing that is to put him in here, [the Murugan Temple] where you're sitting now.

So this is something we have planned for. We've got all the materials just outside the door. We are going to board up the windows, put plastic on the floor, put boards down, put straw around the walls, protect the shuttered areas. Take the doors off here, and we're going to decorate it. It's going to be a Nandi temple.

We're going to have beautiful saris all around the thing. We're going to set up a shrine in the front. We have one of the little green tents out there with chairs for the devotees and we will have pujas here every day. It will be a Nandi temple. It's part of Lord Siva's temple, Lord Subramanium, and if they want to come and kill him, then they'll have to desecrate a Hindu temple to do that. They might think

twice before they just storm in here with a big van load of police to do that.

There's no 9 o'clock puja tonight, if Swami Ramakrishna could do the lamps—you can keep the gopuram closed, do the lamps and explain to the Lord what we're doing. I'm sure He would be very supportive, because, you know, that's what it's all about, isn't it? The most sacred thing for Skanda Vale is the sanctity of life.

This is everything that Guru's whole teaching is about. It's about the divinity embodied in all of life and the sanctity of life. And we have to do everything in our power to uphold that, uphold the cornerstone of dharma— Sanatana Dharma.

THIS PAGE: Transcript of a talk by Swami Suryananda, shortly after Shambo tested positive for TB. **NEXT PAGE:** Community and devotees create a secure pen for Shambo in the back of the Murugan Temple.

FIONA BRUCE, BBC REPORTER: Hindus from across Britain are threatening to form a human chain to prevent the slaughter of a bull, which has tested positive for bovine TB. The animal, named Shambo, is kept at a Hindu temple near Carmarthen in South West Wales. Devotees say they're determined to oppose the slaughter notice because the killing of cows and bulls is against their religion.

ROBERT PIGOTT, BBC REPORTER: Skanda Vale Monastery celebrates the presence of God in living things. Cattle such as Shambo, the community's sacred bull, are particularly honoured. But Shambo has tested positive for TB and the Welsh Assembly Government insists he must be slaughtered. The community says that's unthinkable.

SWAMI BRAHMANANDA: His life is a sacred gift and he has as much right to it as any human being. That is the law of God and Skanda Vale is a place where that law will be upheld.

RIGHT: Shambo, BBC News, 09.05.2007.

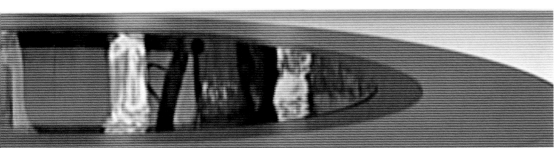

ROBERT PIGOTT: It would be almost impossible to overstate just how precious Shambo is to this community. They'd no more consider killing him than a member of their own family. It's just the latest in a series of clashes between freedom of religion and the law of the land; conflicts which are increasingly being decided in favour of secular values. Like the monastery's cattle, its elephant, Valli, would never be killed. Just like them, she'll die of old age. But veterinary officials say they can't take risks with TB:

CHRISTIANNE GLOSSOP, WALES CHIEF VETERINARY OFFICER: This is a chronic, debilitating disease, and any animal which we believe to be infected, that we just simply leave to develop, the symptoms, would really be regarded as a serious welfare issue.

ROBERT PIGOTT: Hindu leaders say they'll bring thousands of people to form a human barrier around Shambo. At stake, they say, is nothing less than the sanctity of life for which their religion stands.

We can never allow any life entrusted to our care to be killed.

SWAMI SURYANANDA: To obey the will of God is one of the most difficult things for people to do in the pressure of today's society but that is what we are doing with Shambo. We have no choice. We can never allow any life entrusted to our care to be killed. He is a member of our family. There is a very simple solution here and that solution is for Jane Davidson, who is the minister in charge of making this decision to realise that Skanda Vale is a place of worship, it is a temple and that Shambo's life is sacred here.

We are not a commercial farm. We never kill any animal. No animal leaves here. He was born here, he will die here naturally. If an animal is sick, we never put that animal down. We work with our vets and we are committed to spending as much money and as much time to care for life. We know what caring for life means. We have cattle here over twenty years old. We have cows that have not been able to stand up for over a year. We know how to care for them, to turn them over, to treat them like you would a person who is terminally ill.

We run a hospice eight miles from here, looking after people who are terminally ill. Our job is serving God in life and the people in government need to realise that that is a different world from a commercial farm whose job is to kill to make money. It's quite a clear difference.

There are many advanced tests and diagnostics available for bovine TB, as there are for TB in human beings. Tuberculosis is treatable in animals; it can be treated in elephants, it can be treated in cows, it can be treated in gorillas, it can be treated in any animal. If you can treat it in a human being you can treat it in an animal. There just has to be the will to do this.

Transcript of Swami Suryananda's temple discourse, 10.06.2007.

GEORGE ALAGIAH, BBC REPORTER: Shambo has been making headlines across the world for months and today was no different when Shambo the bullock who tested positive for bovine tuberculosis was spared from slaughter by a high court judge. In this 50 page judgement, he ruled that slaughtering Shambo would amount to a gross interference of the monks religious freedoms under the European Convention on Human Rights. His Honour, Judge Hickenbottom, added that the Assembly Government had failed to balance those rights with the need to protect public health.

Barristers for the Assembly Government left without commenting, but an urgent appeal has been allowed and will be heard on Friday. The government says it's disappointed with today's decision.

DAI DAVIES, NATIONAL FARMERS UNION: You say it can be treated, other scientists would say it can't be treated. I'm bitterly disappointed because it drives a cart and horses through the only tool we have to combat this disease.

RIGHT: Shambo, BBC Wales, 16.07.2007. Community members outside the High Court in Cardiff, and back at Skanda Vale, celebrate the verdict.

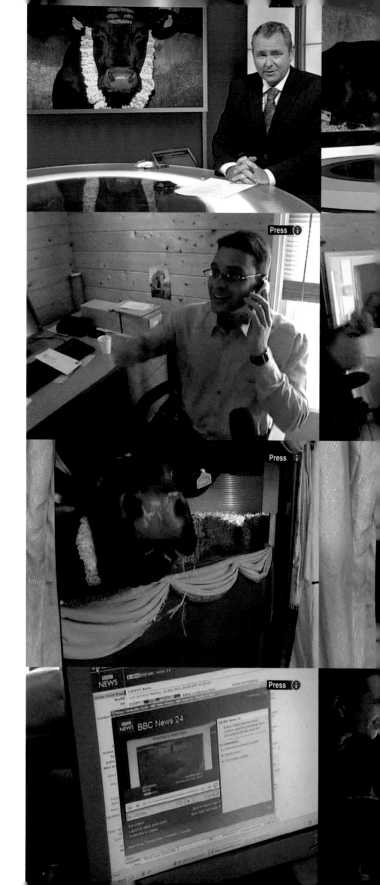

PENNY ROBERTS
BBC WALES TODAY
Chief Reporter

openreach
BT

Press ⓘ

263

DAI DAVIES
NFU Cymru

BBC NEWS

SWAMI GOVINDA: At the appeal court in London, three judges presided over Shambo's fate. The first judge acknowledged that the slaughter of Shambo would be a gross infringement on our human right to exercise our religious beliefs; a glimmer of hope. 'However', he said... and our stomachs dropped. Everything else was hanging on the second judge's statement. He opened his mouth and said, 'I agree.' We knew then that we had lose the case.

SWAMI BRAHMANANDA: They will have to physically desecrate a temple to get him. We will be having an act of worship in front of where he is. If the Welsh Assembly Government want to take him out of there, they will have to interrupt an act of worship. Our religious laws prevent us from assisting in the killing of any life and so we will not help the inspectors remove Shambo.

SIAN LLOYD, BBC REPORTER: As we come on air, officials are preparing to take away Shambo the bullock to be slaughtered. Earlier, police moved into the Skanda Vale Temple in Carmarthenshire to forcibly remove protesters who were trying to protect him. Animal health inspectors served a warrant there after Shambo had tested positive for bovine TB. Well, let's get the latest now from our chief reporter, Penny Roberts, who's there. Penny, over to you for the latest.

PENNY ROBERTS, BBC REPORTER: Sian, thank you very much. You join us amid remarkable scenes. You can probably see behind us here the line of police. They entered the temple just after four o'clock and spent many hours removing people who were praying there from the temple.

They are now in the heart of the temple which houses Shambo, and all the time the rhythmic chanting continues, proclaiming the sanctity of life. These are people whose beliefs mean they will not countenance violence, but their policy of non-cooperation is proving just as problematic for the police and for the authorities.

You'll remember that Shambo tested positive for TB. The monks here in Skanda Vale regard all life as sacred. They believe Shambo is sacred. They believe in the sanctity of life. They went to the High Court, and they managed to win their case, saying that the Assembly Government should not have put a slaughter notice on Shambo. That went to the Court of Appeal in London on Monday, and that decision was overturned.

Even though we ultimately lost the case at the Court of Appeal, all our legal fees were paid by the government.

SWAMI SURYANANDA: Back in 2004, Shambo had tested 'inconclusive', and at the time Guru had said two things: Firstly, he told me to get legal advice. He said, 'This is about the Right to Worship,' and he kept on going on about the Human Rights Act. So, we engaged Bindmans, one of the country's top human rights solicitors, to represent us.

They wrote a letter to DEFRA reminding them of their duty under Article 9 of the Human Rights Act not to act in a way that would constitute an infringement on our right to practise our religion. So, as soon as the drama kicked off in 2007, we already had excellent solicitors with a history of our case.

The second thing which Guru said back then was, 'If they threaten any of our animals, put them in the temple.' So, even though Guru was physically unavailable when the drama started, he had already shown us that, one: we should protect Shambo in the temple; and, two: we should construct a case based upon the fact that Shambo's slaughter would be a gross infringement on our human right to express our 'religion,' as founded on Sanatana Dharma, where the core principle is the sanctity of life.

Establishing Skanda Vale—there are always challenges and dramas. It is never going to be easy. But Guru taught us how to harness and use the energy of God to be successful.

Key dramas—challenges that threatened Skanda Vale's existence or core values—they have always unfolded according to a divine timetable. Whether it was court cases, meetings or outcomes, the key dates always synchronise with the intensity of our worship and festivals.

People think divine experience is about seeing Krishna materializing in front of them—bright lights and so forth. Yes, that is one experience of the Divine. But when you learn to work with and use the energy of God for the benefit of humanity—well, that's another side. Then you begin to see all of these challenges and difficulties as dramas directed by the Divine.

Shambo was a divine drama. The way that key events played out; the timing was so extraordinary. You know, Guru died literally within an hour of Shambo's slaughter notice being issued.

That slaughter notice enabled a judicial review, so our solicitors could get a guarantee from the government that they would not come to try and take Shambo whilst that review was in process. It gave us complete freedom to focus on Guru's burial at the Samadhi. We closed the temples for a whole week and buried him without having to worry that the government were going to tip up with the police and try and break Shambo out of the temple.

So, we had one week to focus on Guru, and as soon as that had finished, it was done and dusted. Everyone had to forget about Guru. There was no time for people to think; 'Oh, there's no Guru, what are we going to do?' There's just no time because we've got this court case.

Then, the actual day they came to take Shambo was the day that we would have had the Royal Shanmukha Mahabhishekam—that's when it would have been. All these things follow the divine calendar. That's how intricately they are intertwined.

SWAMI GOVINDA: The morning after Shambo died, we completely dismantled his pen, cleaned up the straw, removed the boards, removed the saris and deep-cleaned the whole space. We were in the middle of the Subramanium Festival, and three days later we were having the Reunion, with Lord Murugan, Valli, and Devani, coming in procession right through the very space where Shambo had been living.

And we really had to pinch ourselves to remember that it had actually only happened three days ago. It seemed like months had elapsed already; that was the speed of the whole process and also the clinical kind of efficiency with which, I suppose, we were working.

That's not to say that we weren't sad—we were devastated—but we'd done everything we could. Shambo had gone; gone with a huge amount of grace, and then we were on to the next thing. It was the end of the Subramanium festival—the highpoint of our year.

Guru dies, Shambo dies, but the festival needs to be fulfilled and it needed to be fulfilled really beautifully and fully. And it actually was; it was immensely powerful.

13. GURU'S LEGACY

I am only the messenger. It is the Lord you must go to, and only the Lord. That is my message to everyone. The biggest headache in my life has been pushing people away from adulation of the guru. It is very common and of no use. I would allow you to have all the adulation you desire for the guru if I was going to live forever and ever, but I will die, like you, like everybody else. And I don't want a vacuum created between me, you, and the Lord. My job is to give you shakti, to remove the obstacles in your life, so that you can take all your baggage and go and meet the Lord. Train your mind to go to God. You have got very many facets of God, beautiful facets of God. What on earth are you doing thinking of me all the time? Forget about me.

In my previous incarnation I was Swami Brahmananda in the Sri Ramakrishna order. When he died, all of those who had been running after him disappeared and it was I, as Brahmananda, who brought them all back and we began to regroup once more.

SWAMI NARAYANA: He said several times, 'Look, I've seen ashrams fall apart when the big man goes—I've seen the Sri Ramakrishna order fall apart.' When he was Swami Brahmananda he had to go around collecting everybody, bringing them back to be part of the Sri Ramakrishna order. And he said he really didn't want that to happen here, so he was stepping back all the time—further and further.

He would always attend the Swamis meetings to begin with, and then little by little, more and more... he wanted the Swamis to stand on their feet and learn how to do it themselves, which they did quite quickly. We've been very lucky with the people here.

LEFT: The monastic disciples of Sri Ramakrishna, with Swami Brahmananda (seated centre).

285

Skanda Vale has come of age, and the members of the Community have developed such a taste for excellence. I love the way everybody is committed and dedicated to what they are doing.

INTERVIEWER: It must have been very challenging, coping with Guru and Shambo at once?

SISTER MARIA: Strangely enough, it was an absolutely wonderful time, an extremely powerful and intense time for the Community. So together in what we were doing. It gave me a lot of confidence in the future of Skanda Vale because sometimes, I used to think, I'm not sure if our monks are mature enough to take over yet. I was a bit worried about that. Only when that drama happened, when the neighbour built a roadblock and we gathered to meet Guru, Swami gave a talk there. And I tell you, that talk he gave, I thought, no question that we will be fine when Guru goes. We will be fine. They will be absolutely ready to take over in a very good way. They know what to do and they have determination. They learnt so much from Guru, it was like they shared the same blood.

SWAMI NARAYANA: Over and over again, the Swami's Council has proven its strength as a structure and as a safeguard against a human's egocentric nature. One person running Skanda Vale would be disastrous and with the Council, you have five pairs of eyes on a situation rather than one. We are essentially responsible for these great temples, these powerhouses which have been established by the Divine here. It's very much our duty to protect that purity and keep it free and available to all.

RIGHT: Formed in 1993, the Swami's Council is a group of senior monks who take responsibility for running Skanda Vale.

SWAMI KARUNA: He used to say 'You will never grow up until I've gone, because while I'm still here, you are always going to lean on me, hide behind me; you do what I ask you to do, but no one really will be making much of an effort to evolve.'

SWAMI KARUNA: And my experience now, of the last fifteen years since Guru died, is how an extraordinary story has unfolded since his physical departure. The way that Skanda Vale is literally pulsating with energy—it's abundant and full of life—you can hear it, feel it, see it.

The birdsong, the lush surroundings, the children playing, the bustle of pilgrims, the Community and devotees working on project after project (after project), people visiting, eating, connecting, serving—everything.

And all without asking for a single penny. Upholding purity, inviting grace. The more people worshipping, the more power Skanda Vale has to give others, and the higher the demand to keep expanding to accommodate that power. People all over the world benefiting from what has been established here with complete and total direction from the Divine.

LEFT: Community members and devotees during the Subramanium Festival, August 2020.

Every day, I look at Skanda Vale and I say to myself,
Gosh, Mother—thank you for this amazing opportunity—
that I have been chosen and given this responsibility
to house You and enable people to come and find
themselves in the silence of their own hearts.
To worship God fearlessly, to serve God, to care for
humanity fearlessly without this hang-up of conversion,
without us putting pressure on your mind to find yourself.
Divine friends, that is our journey here. For in this
kaliyuga, the age of destruction—the lack of discipline,
the lack of orderliness, the lack of direction—we have
to lead people, we cannot be led, we cannot follow other
people and just blindly follow.

GLOSSARY

MURUGAN

Born among reeds in a celestial lake, Murugan is Sara-vana-bhava. For six days, he was nursed by the six Krttika (the Pleiades), wives of Agni, and so he is known as Karttikeya. With six faces as Shanmukha, he surveys the six planes of consciousness and encompasses their totality. He embodies the transcendent seventh known as Satyam—Truth, or Reality.

As Devasenapati, he is the commander-in-chief of the three worlds who wields the Vel—the great spear of wisdom, knowledge, and discrimination. With it, Murugan does battle with demonic forces, including the mighty Surapadman; the epitome of ego.

Murugan represents the power of wisdom (jnana-shakti) and is flanked by his consorts, Valli and Devani, daughters of the Earth and Heavens; the cosmic powers of action (kriya-shakti) and will (iccha-shakti), respectively. Along with his consorts, Murugan comprises the three in one, the one in three—Bhur, Bhuvah Svah—together expressed as AUM.

SHAKTI

Maha Shakti is unbound primordial nature; the creative and transformative power of the cosmos. She is the dynamic feminine aspect of the Supreme Divine and holds within herself infinite potential. Intent on self-expression, Shakti represents the urge to create, and so it is She who excites Consciousness to become manifest.

As Her nature is all-encompassing, Shakti transcends all preconceived notions of duality. She appears both serene and terrifying, immaculate and wild, light and dark. Both Lakshmi and Kali are Her forms. Ultimately, She is playful and delights in Her apparent contrariness. This is Her Maya, the very principle of manifestation, which invites us to draw near and know Her reality. She is Mother.

RANGANATHA

In the form of Ranganatha, Vishnu lies recumbent upon the great celestial serpent, Adishesha, also known as Ananta (the Eternal). He sleeps on the bed of eternity and floats, dreaming his way through the Cosmic Ocean. The undulating motion of Adishesha is the movement of the entire universe, time and space. As he uncoils, Creation unfolds, and as he recoils the world withdraws.

Ranganatha is the Lord of Preservation, presiding over the cyclical nature of all things. At the moment when the universe is made manifest, the four-headed Lord Brahma emerges from Ranganatha's navel as the great Creator, giving life and vibrancy to the cosmos.

Lakshmi sits alongside Ranganatha as his consort. She is also his inherent power (Shakti); his feminine equivalent without which Vishnu cannot act or even dream. Hanuman, standing upright with folded palms, attends to his Lord with unswerving devotion.

Glory to He in the form of Brahma, who creates; in Your steadfast Universal form (Vishnu), You preserve. In the form of Rudra (Siva), You destroy a Universal age— Glory to You of three forms!

AGAMA SASTRA: a branch of Hindu scriptures that provide detailed instructions and guidelines for rituals, worship, temple construction, and spiritual practices.

AARTI: the ritual of worship in which a flame, accompanied by the singing of devotional songs, is offered to a deity. It involves circling a lamp or fire in a clockwise direction.

ASHRAM: a hermitage, monastic community, or spiritual retreat where individuals engage in spiritual practices.

AVATAR: the incarnation or manifestation of a deity or divine being on Earth. Avatars descend to fulfil a specific purpose, restore balance, and guide humanity.

BHAJAN: a devotional song or hymn, often sung by a congregation of devotees.

BHAKTI: devotion and love towards the Divine with an emphasis on a personal relationship with God through prayer, worship, and surrender.

BHAKTI YOGA: a spiritual method that emphasises the cultivation of devotion and love.

BRAHMA: one of the principal deities in Hinduism. He is the creator of the universe often depicted with four heads, each representing a Veda, and is associated with knowledge and creation.

DARSHAN: the act of seeing or beholding a deity, revered person, or sacred object. It also refers to the reciprocal act of the deity or person bestowing blessings and grace upon the devotee through their gaze.

DATTATREYA: an incarnation of the combined form of the divine trinity—Brahma, Vishnu, and Siva.

DHARMA: a fundamental concept that encompasses moral and ethical duties, righteousness, and the cosmic order.

DURGA: often depicted as a warrior goddess riding a lion or tiger. She represents protection, strength, and the triumph of good over evil.

GANESHA: the elephant-headed God, revered as the remover of obstacles, the patron of arts and sciences, and the deity of wisdom and intellect.

GANGA: the most sacred river in Hinduism. Believed to have divine origins, the river is worshipped as a goddess and is associated with spiritual liberation and purity.

GOPURAM: the monumental entrance tower or gateway of a South Indian temple, though Guru Sri Subramanium used the term to refer to a temple's sanctum sanctorum (conventionally referred to as a garbhagriha).

GURU PURNIMA: an annual festival celebrated in honour of spiritual and academic teachers. It falls on the full moon day of the Hindu month of Asadha.

HANUMAN: Lord Rama's monkey companion, revered as an archetype of devotion, courage, and loyalty.

KALASAM: a metal or stone finial used to top the domes of temples. The term can also refer to a ceremonial pot or vessel used in rituals and worship (see kumbha).

KALIYUGA: the final and current age in the cycle of four ages (yugas) according to Hindu cosmology. It is characterised by a decline in dharmic values and spiritual awareness.

KALIYUGA AVATARA: an incarnation of a deity or divine being specifically for the purpose of restoring righteousness and spiritual upliftment during the kaliyuga.

KARMA: the universal law of cause and effect, which also governs the consequences of one's actions.

KARMA YOGA: the path of selfless action and service, which emphasises the performance of one's duties and responsibilities without attachment to the results; offering the fruits of all actions to the Divine.

KRISHNA: the eighth avatara of Lord Vishnu. He is revered for his teachings in the Bhagavad Gita and is often depicted playing a flute as a divine charmer and cowherd.

KUMBHA: a ceremonial pot used especially during festive occasions.

KUMKUM: a fragrant red powder made from turmeric. It is applied as a mark in the centre of the forehead, symbolising auspiciousness and spiritual awakening.

LAKSHMI: the goddess of wealth, prosperity, and abundance. She is the divine consort of Lord Vishnu.

LOKA: a realm or plane of existence in Hindu cosmology, representing different dimensions of reality, including the physical world (bhuloka) and higher celestial realms (svargaloka etc.).

MAHABHARATA: one of the two major ancient Sanskrit epics of Hindu literature, the other being the Ramayana. It narrates the epic story of the Kuru dynasty, including the Kurukshetra War, and contains the Bhagavad Gita.

MAHABHISEKAM: ritually anointing and bathing an image of a deity with sacred substances.

MANDALA: an intricate geometric pattern that represents the cosmos. Different variations are employed in meditation and visualisation rituals as an aid for focusing the mind.

MANTRA: a sacred sound, syllable, word, or phrase that is repeated or chanted as a form of spiritual practice (see japa).

MATA KALI: or Mother Kali—the ultimate form of Devi, often terrifying in appearance. She represents time, the transcendence of impermanence, annihilation of the ego and ultimate liberation, or moksha.

MURTI: a sacred image or statue of a deity, which is a physical representation of the Divine.

NARAYANA: a name of Lord Vishnu, representing his divine form as the supreme deity. It signifies the cosmic aspect of Vishnu as the sustainer and preserver of the universe.

PRASADAM: sacred food that has been offered to and blessed by a deity. It is distributed to devotees after worship.

PUJA: ritual worship, often involving the offering of prayers, flowers, incense, and other sacred items to invoke the presence and blessings of the Divine.

PUJARI: a person who conducts religious rituals, ceremonies, and pujas.

RAMA: an incarnation of Lord Vishnu and the central character of the epic Ramayana. He is revered for his righteousness, courage, and adherence to dharma.

RASMI: rays of light or radiance, representing the divine effulgence or luminous energy that emanates from a deity or an enlightened being. Guru Sri Subramanium often used the term in the sense of 'Divine providence'—that is, the capacity of the Divine to provide whatever is required.

RISHI: a sage or seer who attains spiritual knowledge through deep meditation and tapas (austerity).

SANKALPA: a resolve or intention. It is a conscious statement of purpose and dedication, aligning one's mind and actions with a specific goal or spiritual aspiration.

SARASVATI: the goddess of knowledge, wisdom, music, arts, and learning. She is revered as the embodiment of speech and creative expression.

SIVA: one of the principal deities in Hinduism, often associated with the qualities of destruction, transformation, and transcendence.

SUBRAMANIUM: another name for Murugan, Skanda, Shanmukha or Kartikeya, the son of Lord Siva and Goddess Parvati. Guruji adopted this name at a young age.

TRYAMBAKAM: an ancient Vedic mantra to Siva 'The Three-Eyed One.'

TAPAS: spiritual austerity, self-discipline, and ascetic penance undertaken by individuals to purify the mind, body, and soul.

VAHANA: the vehicle or mount associated with a deity. It represents the deity's qualities and powers. For example, Lord Siva's vahana is Nandi, the bull.

VIBHUTI: also referred to as bhasma, is sacred ash that is often applied on the body and particularly associated with Lord Siva. It serves as a symbol of transcendence beyond material impermanence.

VISHNU: one of the principal deities in Hinduism, often regarded as the preserver and protector of the universe.

VISHNU LOKA: also known as Vaikuntha, is the celestial abode or realm of Lord Vishnu. It is considered a divine realm of supreme bliss and eternal peace, where devotees of Vishnu reside after attaining liberation, or moksha.

YAAGAM: also known as yajna, is a ritual offering to the sacred fire (agni). It involves reciting mantras, making offerings and invoking deities to purify the environment and promote spiritual growth.

YOGESHWARA: An epithet of Siva as Lord of Yoga.

'The Spark Becomes Fire' shares stories of Guru Sri Subramanium's work and life primarily in and around Skanda Vale, and yet a large part of his activities were focussed outside the Ashram; at Skanda Vale Hospice and Somaskanda Temple in Switzerland. A forthcoming second book will focus on stories from those projects, and all that has unfolded between 2007 and the present day.